Gospel Realities

How the Kingdom of God Shapes Reality

Chase Alan O'Dell

Gospel Realities: How the Kingdom of God Shapes Reality

Copyright © 2018 by Chase A. O'Dell
All rights reserved.

Scripture quotations are from the ESV® Bible (The Holy Bible, English Standard Version®), copyright © 2001 by Crossway, a publishing ministry of Good News Publishers. Used by permission. All rights reserved." Scripture quotations taken from the New American Standard Bible® (NASB). Copyright © 1960, 1962, 1963, 1968, 1971, 1972, 1973, 1975, 1977, 1995 by The Lockman Foundation. Used by permission. www.Lockman.org. Scripture quotations marked (NIV) are taken from the Holy Bible, New International Version®, NIV®. Copyright © 1973, 1978, 1984, 2011 by Biblica, Inc. ™ Used by permission of Zondervan. All rights reserved worldwide. www.zondervan.com The "NIV" and "New International Version" are trademarks registered in the United States Patent and Trademark Office by Biblica, Inc. ™

ISBN -10: 1983755532
ISBN -13: 978-1983755538

This book is to all those that God has inserted into my story. To God be the glory for this book, which is His story. To my parents, my wife Tara, and my children. To my brothers that God has used as instruments for His glory in my story. To all those that have come alongside me and to those that have come against me. You have all been an integral part of the making of this story.

Contents

Introduction 1

Chapter 1: Remember When...7

Chapter 2: Some Things You Can't Control..................................9

Chapter 3: Dark New Reality 17

Chapter 4: Controlling What You Can't Control.......................29

Chapter 5: The Night Gets Darker 47

Chapter 6: No Way Out...55

Chapter 7: Back to Square One..59

Chapter 8: Home Sweet Home 65

Chapter 9: Uncertainty and the Presence of God 69

Chapter 10: The Only Way Out..79

Chapter 11: A New Perspective 89

Chapter 12: Baby Steps..93

Chapter 13: The Doctrine of Reality 101

Chapter 14: Learning to Run 105

Chapter 15: Relearning Intimacy 117

Chapter 16: A Living Story...123

Chapter 17: New You = New Goal 131

Conclusion 149

Notes..151

Introduction

"All that I have written seems like straw to me."[1] Thomas Aquinas, an early church theologian and author, said this after having received a revelation from God that so impacted him, he quit writing. Something he had seen about God had made such a dent in his soul that no words being produced from his writing could illustrate, or even come close to illustrating the magnitude of the reality of God Himself. I find this to be true about myself from time to time.

At the time of this writing, I am a pastor in a small church, in a small town, with a small pedigree, and with a small realm of influence. None of these things deter me from expressing what I know to be true of God. The only problem with me talking about God is that everything I write just seems to fall short. I preach on a weekly basis. Every Sunday morning is another opportunity to declare God's greatness. Some people are gripped, and some people are not. Does this have anything to do with me? Yes and no.

Currently I am twenty-seven and have been preaching for a few years now. I have traveled to different country churches around the Kansas City area. Some were gripped by my message, no matter how long or short, or how skilled or unskilled, and some fell asleep. I would imagine if God were to suddenly show up and reveal His greatness Himself, those who were gripped and those who were asleep would probably instantly fall on the floor in worship. They would all leave forever changed. This has yet to happen, so in the meantime, I am the middleman for God's greatness. I do my best to listen to the Holy Spirit, articulate, illustrate, and surrender to the power of the Spirit in my sermons while I preach. Though this is true, I am the middle man, who just happens to look like a man, dress like one, tell jokes that aren't always funny like one, and go a little bit too long when I preach like one.

I am trying to illustrate to a group of people a new reality that they may not be aware of. I do not always teach something new to everybody. Sometimes they may be hearing what they already know, at least on an intellectual level, but the way it hits them is new. They may be a card-carrying Christian for years, demonstrated by the regular Sunday school attendance, choir performances, regular church attendance, or how many times they took one for the team and volunteered to serve in the toddler ministry. A new reality of a gospel truth may hit them, demolishing some pain, some struggle, and some limited way of thinking forever. This of course, is not me. This is what the Holy Spirit can do. If not for him, I might be able to stand up and tell a few jokes—many of which would not be funny—and that would be that.

When the Holy Spirit speaks, He makes the truth relevant to you. Though something may have always been truth, it makes its way to you through relevance and now becomes a truth to you. You and truth become joined together. It is a beautiful picture of intimacy, considering Jesus himself said, "I am the way, and the truth, and the life..." (John 14:6). One day we will be at a wedding feast with Him, where the ultimate way two people can come together-marriage- becomes a reality between Jesus and us. The institution of marriage is an illustration of a much greater reality; it is a picture, a living and breathing work of art of the union of a believer in Christ and Christ Himself. That is the difference between my preaching and the preaching of Jesus. Jesus can create something living and breathing, that talks and walks, that fights and argues, that makes love and destroys it, that fights over the remote and where they are going to eat for dinner, and use it to illustrate a much larger cosmic truth, one that bends the very intellectual capacities and weighs down the emotional scales of any man. I am limited to words. Do you see the difference?

So here is what I will offer you. I will offer you a depiction of a living and breathing illustration with words. I will use my life to show you God's great sermon if you will, about a much larger truth that is bigger than you or I. You have no interest in my life? I don't ask that to sound cynical but just to be real about how we really think, and if you don't then that's fine. I'm sure my life is similar in many ways to yours. I look up at the same sky as you, I have the same types of issues with others that you may have, the same selfish thoughts, the same temptations, the same short-sightedness about life, the same hard heartedness and the same pondering questions. One such question is this: "What is so special about my life?"

You get up, go to work, come home, eat dinner, play with kids if you have them, watch T.V. if you have time, and go to bed Repeat, repeat, repeat. Your life may not look like that, but no matter how great or how small you think you are, you still run up against many of the same issues that the rest of us do because you are human. What if I were to tell you that those seemingly mundane events of your life could have huge significance? You don't always have to change what you are doing to see the significance in your life; you just have to see things the way God does, and what you do as a result will determine the outcome.

There are many occasions where I cry out to God that I don't belong here. I don't belong in this world with its value system, its culture, its way of looking at things. I don't fit in, and I don't fit out. I am an alien and the more time I spend with God, the more my perspective or what I do on a daily basis seems irrelevant because of what the weight of eternity reveals about them. This may sound depressing, but I assure you, it is perfectly natural. This is part of learning to acknowledge that as believers we are "...strangers and exiles on the earth" (Hebrews 11:13). The fact that we are "strangers" shows us that we are stranger than those around us. You see, these cries are not cries of sadness, nor are they cries of hopelessness, but they stem from the very large hope that is within me. That doesn't make sense to some of you, I understand. Seven or eight years ago it

Introduction

wouldn't have made sense to me either. That being said, this is a good place to start my journey.

Gospel Realities

Chapter 1
Remember When

I grew up in a Christian household, I was born into Christianity, if you will. Before you pull the heresy alarm, hear me out. My parents were both imperfect Christians, and had to travel a distance on their own journey with God before I came on to the scene. I am the middle of three sons. That makes me the superstar right? Not quite, but my parents loved me deeply. I was immersed in church from birth. Obviously, I don't remember, but I can imagine the prayers that surrounded me as a baby. Children's Bible stories were a part of my day-to-day existence as I sucked my thumb and pooped in my diaper.

There was something unique about me as a child. Eventually, as most of us do, I grew out of the diaper and slobbering stage and into the talking and walking stage. Even at four and five years old, I had a dynamic relationship with God. I would talk with God and I was told I would tell people how God talked back. I don't remember what He said, but whatever it was it stuck with people. Many people, including my great-grandma Alta, who had to have been in her seventies at the time, said I would one day grow up to be a pastor. Something about me illustrated that to people.

Gospel Realities

Many things about the rest of my life were pretty average besides that. I liked to ride my bike, get beat up by my older brother, and play video games. I swam on the swim team, where I was good for my age, but not great. I played a little bit of flag football and stunk at it; I was the kid who ran the ball to my own end zone. So there was nothing of great significance besides my relationship with God. That was one identifying marker in my life that seemed to separate me from many others.

Chapter 2
Some Things You Can't Control

There are lifestyles and ways of thinking that many of us are just born into. None of us chose our family, our race, our birthplace, our family religion, or how much money our parents made. None of us chose whether we would have one, two, or any parents. We didn't get to choose whether they were nice or abusive, smart or stupid, funny or bland, hardworking or lazy. We didn't get to choose, our birth order, who our brothers or sisters were, or whether or not they would treat us nice. We didn't get to decide whether our family would be functional or dysfunctional, loving or cold, relational or isolated, or involved or uncaring. None of those we got to choose, yet many of these factors helped shape us into who we are today. Some of us want to separate ourselves from that notion. Some of us work hard to deny to ourselves or to others where we came from, while some embrace it.

No one can tell me that an abusive father hasn't shaped the way we view our girlfriend, boyfriend, husband, or wife. If he was a jerk, we can either be that same type of jerk, or we can try to swing the pendulum to the other side and be outwardly very kind, while feeling very vulnerable on the inside. We live with the tension that

Gospel Realities

comes with our background. That is our reality and we are dropped into it. Those things we perceive as truth, become our truth.

If we grow up in a harsh, disengaged household, we grow up thinking the world is cold or indifferent. If we grow up in a loving household where we could depend on our parents, we grow up thinking the world is inviting, with endless possibilities, where people can be trusted. No matter where we come from, we are shaped in some way, by that place. Our limited perspective as young people tells us that this is just "reality." The issues and all the fun and the problems come into play because we all come from different backgrounds. We all have a different way of viewing the world. It just so happens that the world is just small enough that our view of reality often collides with another's view of reality. If we all had completely different backgrounds, we would all feel like we were an American waking up in China every day. Everything would be overwhelmingly different. So our realities are alike and different at the same time.

As we grow up and spend enough time clashing with others and experiencing different things, our view of reality matures. It always changes. This is a good thing. This is what changes the perspective of a baby to a man. We have to be refined or we will never adapt. We will be stuck. Many times something, or someone, will happen in our lives that causes us to get stuck in our perspective. Sometimes that abusive drunken dad never quite leaves the back of our minds. That affair never quite leaves our perspective and we can never really get over it. Our thoughts are invaded by the fear that everyone is devious, that no one is to be trusted. This is called getting stuck. It becomes as difficult as getting our car out of the mud. Sometimes we can push it out, but sometimes we have to get it pulled out. Some mud is so deep though, that no matter how strong we are, or how many people we have in that car, we cannot push it out. Someone has to pull us out.

This is what God does with us. We grow up with different backgrounds, with all these different factors in our life that shape our reality, but our "reality" may not be the truth. Just because you were abused, doesn't mean you are less than human, and just because you cheated or were cheated on, doesn't mean you are worthless and aren't good enough. These times in our lives, whether easy or difficult, can serve as opportunities. They are opportunities for us to get so sick of those realities that we want to throw them out, but we may not know how to do that. This is where Jesus intervenes in our life.

When I was growing up I used to go out on my driveway with my telescope with my Dad to look up at the stars. I guess I was just enamored of something so large. The truth is, whether we believe in God or not, the universe teaches us that there is much more out there than we know about. Space was just so captivating and beautiful to me. I dreamed of one day being out there as an astronaut and getting to be where those stars were. I wanted to be in that world.

Gospel Realities

I used to play a lot of video games growing up, and I mean a lot. I am talking the amount that would leave a permanent imprint of your butt in your chair kind of a lot. I was so captivated by these fantasy worlds that I could spend hours and hours there. I always liked adventure games, where there was a giant world to explore. I was captivated by those worlds so much I would forget about mine. I think that is the appeal of video games. No one inherently likes staring at a screen for hours and hours unless they are captivated by what they see there. A little boy's sense of adventure can spark this. This is not unique to boys alone though. Little girls like to play house, where they have this imaginary family, where Prince Charming is their husband. They have these wonderful, cute children, and this wonderful imaginary life. They are taken to a new world by the power of their imagination. A lot of times we lose this imagination because it clashes with the reality of what we like to call the "real world." We put imagination to the side and call it irrelevant. What is funny is that some of the leading innovators in science, technology, healthcare, and space exploration are those that have the biggest imagination. Their imagination is what drives them forward.

Imagination is something that God gives us as a gift, but we often allow that to become diminished. The Bible is full of word pictures that God intended to use to activate our imagination to present to us a spiritual reality. Revelation chapter four is a good example of this. God presents Himself there to us in such splendor we could have never thought of this on our own. The Bible is not the

Some Things You Can't Control

only book to do this, however. This imagination is where the power of a novel is found. Without an imagination, the stories that novels present would be a bland map of words on a page whose stories become irrelevant, but with an imagination they become alive, because we can see, smell, touch, and taste what the author describes. Sometimes we are even transported right into the midst of that story.

Even in my youth, there was something in me that longed for something more. Whether I viewed it through the telescope or watched it on a screen, I wanted to be a part of a different world. Even at a young age, we have the capacity to know there is something more. We have the capacity to look beyond our reality and be caught up somewhere else. We have built within us, the capacity to know our reality is small compared to what is really out there, and we have the longing within us to want to be a part of that. This is no coincidence. King David in the Psalms declares, "For you created my inmost being; you knit me together in my mother's womb" (Psalm 139:13, NIV). God took delicate care in creating you, despite whatever someone else may have told you. God also knows the exact capacities that He has put within you.

This not only relates to where we want to be in life, but when we want to be there. Our entire lives run on time, at least in America. We live by a schedule. My church starts promptly at 10:30 a.m. If you are not there, we love you, but we won't wait for you. If an employer tells you to be at work by 6:30 a.m. every morning and you violate that enough, there will be consequences. The same is true of the length of our lives. We are born, we live x amount of years, and then we die. As much as we may not want to think about the dying part, we understand that part, at least on an intellectual level. We also realize there are consequences for our time running out. The importance of time has been wired within us. Some operate on a different system than others, but we value it. That's why it is so hard to imagine time running out on us. Death to man is essentially the concept of his time running out, which means his life runs out. All the things we did or wanted to do operate in this system. Many fear death and some do not, but the reality is the same for us, no matter what our perspective of it is. For the Christian time runs out as well, but his existence doesn't.

    Man's way of viewing things is very limited. Time puts us on a twenty-four hour timetable. Businesses open at 9 and close at 5, or whatever time. What if we could know that that won't always be the case? What if there came a point where we could operate on whatever timetable we wanted to, for as long as we wanted to? This concept of timelessness can otherwise be termed "eternity." Eternity is the expansion of time so much that time's limitations do not impede us anymore. The concept of time would not hold any power over our life. What if death was no longer able to steal time from you? What if death bothers us so much because that wasn't part of our original capacities? What if we were not meant to carry the weight of that reality colliding head on with us one day? What if the sadness of it, or the "sting" (1 Corinthians 15:56) is an illustration for us that we weren't made for it.

Man was made to eat, rest, and play. Those things are not burdensome on their own. We operate naturally in those things. We don't have to conjure up the need to eat. If we lack the desire, that tells us something is wrong. It is within us naturally to do those things. Death was not. That is why eternity appeals to us, because we were created for it. The very fact that we conceptualize, talk about it, have many religions that try to reach it, and we become hopeless without it is because we were created for it. It is within our natural capacities to embrace eternity. God has "set eternity in the human heart" (Ecclesiastes 3:11, NIV). We long for it; we reach for it. The idea of other worlds in space, video games, playing house, and unlimited time appeal to us because we were created for those very things. Anything other than that is an abomination to us. C.S. Lewis once said, "If I find in myself a desire which no experience in this world can satisfy, the most probable explanation is that I was made for another world."[2] The very fact that this desire exists within us testifies to the fact that we are aliens in this world.

Gospel Realities

Chapter 3
Dark New Reality

The story does not end there. For many of us, an average American childhood is just the beginning. There came a point in my life where my reality came into collision with another reality I was unaware of. There was a dark world. There was a hurting world. There was a lonely world out there and I didn't know it until I was forced to try to reconcile with its side effects. My older brother Bret is seven years older than I am, and there came a time after a few years of harmony and flag football games, when he was off to college.

My brother is smart, intelligent, very successful in any endeavor in his career, and very personable, so he does not fit the average stereotype for what I am about to tell you. When my brother first enrolled in college, due to insecurity, a new sense of freedom, and grappling with the effects of his new reality, he developed a drug problem. It is funny how many people call marijuana a gateway drug. This may be true, but that is only half the truth. The real gateway into drugs is hurts, heartaches, and emptiness. The drugs become a way to either solve or sedate the problem.

This is where he found himself. In the midst of a new reality, and a new chapter in his life, he saw drugs as a way to smooth the

Gospel Realities

bumpy road of his journey. It began with marijuana and pills, like many others do, and he found his way into cocaine and ecstasy, along with whatever amount of alcohol would give him a release from the world he found himself in. Ironically, what Bret thought drugs would give him, they actually took from him.

All of the problems that had led to using drugs became magnified as the drug use continued. Anybody who knows a drug addict can tell you that drugs never are a one person problem. Drugs have a way of calling out to a person as a result of issues in a family, and eventually drag that same family into the new problems created by the drugs. Our family was no exception.

As young as I was, I was sheltered from many of these issues. Though no one told me what the issues were, I felt their side effects. A problem like that does not creep into a family's house, plop down on the couch, and not affect the atmosphere around it. Out of necessity, my parents began to devote much of their attention to my brother. I was thrown into a new reality, without really understanding what was going on. Though I wasn't an adult, I did what so many adults do—I tried to fix it on my own. My twelve-year-old self tried to heal myself of the effects of a systemic problem that has been plaguing our world for a very long time. Obviously I didn't know what I was doing, and obviously I failed.

I didn't know why, but I knew I was not receiving the attention I once knew, so I looked for wherever I could to find it. At twelve years of age, one of the best ways to get attention is to get yourself in trouble. So that's what I did. Middle school was a new arena to do that in. It had new and exciting ways to get the attention I craved. Acting out in school not only made me popular in a bad way, but it got laughs. Most importantly, it got my drug: attention. The problem with any drug is that it calls out for more within you. It is never satisfied. I would like to tell you I dabbled behavior for a while, had some sort of epiphany, and then moved on from this childhood curse, but it would take many more years before that would happen. Many principal's office visits, detentions, and suspensions later, I found myself kicked out of my middle school.

Now the journey began to find a new school. There was another local school in town that my parents enrolled me. This time it was a Christian school. At this point in my life, the only relationship with God I had was one of apathy. The problems of my pain made me turn my attention away from God and onto attempting to fix this problem that couldn't be fixed with the tools that I had. So, when I enrolled in this school, the idea of it being Christian neither appealed or repelled me. It was just "whatever." A fresh start sounded good though. A "fresh start," however, didn't mean my problems remained in the past; they came with me. I got off the plane and carried that luggage with me.

This school was different. It was much more strict and my desire to get attention from getting in trouble got harder. Now the very notion of trouble was shot down very quickly. This was very frustrating. We had to sit in cubicles and work on a curriculum that

Gospel Realities

was self-planned, and self-directed, and we couldn't speak to each other besides at lunch, recess, and short periods of free time in class. This left me all alone with my mind. Anybody knows that too much time spent in a murky and hurting mind is a bad thing. I remember sitting there thinking for hours on end about all sorts of things. As time went on, my mind became more warped and the emptiness in me grew. I had all this time to think, and no way to release. As I continued to let myself be warped in this way, my hatred towards God grew.

I felt like God was shoved down my throat at school, at home, and at the church I was forced to go to. It felt like God was presented to me as the only cure for any ailment. The feeling I had was that if only I could sign on to whatever it was I was supposed to sign on to with God then I would be cured and I would finally meet everyone's expectations. I would finally be good enough for everybody. It seemed like the only attention I could get was someone looking down on me and telling me to straighten up. This only made this tension within me grow. I wanted this hurt to be healed in me.

My brother had gotten to a point that, though his personal life was still dysfunctional, he no longer wanted to kill himself. That situation began to coast on its own, though the damage to me had already been done. No one seemed to give me the attention that I wanted, and when they did, it always seemed to be related to this God. There was a point in my pain during this period that I cried out to him and I could feel His presence and peace for a little while, but after a little bit of time, I fell away from Him. The pain kept creeping up in my life. My mind became more warped as I felt the tension of my problem increase, with no release.

When a pipe gets clogged up enough, it will either leak or explode. I was to do a little bit of both soon enough.

All I could think about was this pain. I was not emotionally equipped enough to identify the problem, and it was not until later on in life when those family problems were revealed to me was I even able to understand. I could not identify it, and I could not take my pain away, so all I did was dwell on it. There was an emotional pain and sense of hopelessness that this problem just intensified. My mind would not stop running all the time, and the only thing that was on it were very dark things, which would affect my emotions and which would affect the way I dealt with people.

No one knew the extent of my pain. No one knew how every few minutes I would think about killing myself. No one knew that I was drowning. My parents only knew I was not the same person they knew as a child. I was growing, but I wasn't maturing-- at least emotionally. I became very introverted. I would spend hours just thinking, and thinking, and thinking, and it was never about anything good. I was so hurt I would never have dared to open up enough to be vulnerable to anyone. I was shut off and hated everyone, but I hated myself the most.

This God everyone spoke of became a new target for my hatred. Everyone spoke of Him as some cure for me. When people

Gospel Realities

would try to speak to me about Him, I would immediately run from the situation. The idea of opening up was unbearable. I felt I had to carry this hatred alone. There was no one who understood and no one that ever could. I hated this God because He was the reason why I couldn't measure up in anyone's eyes. This God was indifferent to me and to my pain. I hated Him so much that I hated Christians as well. I hated their happiness and how they didn't pursue sin like me. They felt totally separate from me. The only people I felt a connection with were people like me. The people who thought darkly like me, who shrugged God off and wanted to get into the same type of trouble as me. Though I felt drawn to them, I still always felt alone.

To my relief I got into enough of the same type of trouble, enough times to get kicked out of that school. Time for another fresh start, I thought. Time to finally be free and get that release I was looking for. I knew a public school would be much easier to do that. I knew I would not feel watched all the time and I felt like I had more opportunity to get into more trouble, which equaled more attention to me. I was right. There was more opportunity to do that here. I took this move to a new school as walking up to the next starting line. I could sprint off this line and finally leave God behind. At this point I was so sick of hearing about this God that I moved past hatred and into indifference.

Immediately I was drawn to people who thought like me, who acted like me, and who didn't care what people thought. I wanted to escape to these type of people because they could help me forget about all that pain and all those Christians behind me. It didn't take long for me to find them. These people were accepting of me. Many of these students I went to elementary school with, but at least in my mind they had forgotten about me after all those years at the Christian school. I didn't want to associate with any of the kids I hung out with then because they reminded me too much of that pain of the past. The people I ran to didn't care what others thought. They didn't really care about school, and they didn't really care about themselves. They said what they wanted, when they wanted, and didn't seem to be limited by rules like the ones I felt were shoved down my throat all time I spent time growing up in a Christian household. They had the freedom to do what they wanted. The best thing was that they helped me forget about my pain and they had no association in my mind with God.

I was about sixteen by this point in my life. My relationship with my parents had pretty much deteriorated from working together to just co-existing. They reminded me of my pain, limiting rules, and, worst of all God, which reminded me of everything else that had hurt me. I would go to and from school, speaking to them as little as possible most days. I would tell them just what they needed to know and get on with it. I would lie to them when I needed to go to a party or whatever sometimes, but most of the time it was just a relationship of co-existing, me getting caught in a lie, getting screamed at and grounded, co-existing some more, and then repeat. My life was

Gospel Realities

beginning to change though; I was entering a new reality, one without God. This was good for me I thought. The further I got away from God, the further I got away from my pain and my hatred.

Around this time, I got a job at a local diner. These were some good times. The job was incredibly easy. I felt like they took me on there as more of a favor to a family member that got me the job than that they actually needed me. I was a bus boy there. The job was not the best part, though; it was the people. The job itself was about as mindless as it gets, but the people were pretty great. After I had been working there a while, they took me in as family. They accepted me and listened to me. They did not force God down my throat, and I felt valued to them. I didn't feel like I never measured up around them.

I spent a lot of time with these people. I was particularly close to three of the other employees there who were around my age. I remember we would talk for hours in the kitchen as the dishwasher—whoever it happened to be for the day—washed the dishes and I delivered them to where they belonged in the front of the diner. I felt like that kitchen was my escape. I felt alone and estranged from everyone else but those that worked there. We talked about whatever it was that was on our minds or in our imaginations, whether it was aliens, zombie invasions, anime, stupid things on the news, the Rolling Stones, or anything else we could think of. I used to get lost in our conversations. I was taken to another world for just a few hours in the evenings and weekends I worked.

At that diner, I was transported to another place, another world, and I was a different person when I was around them. I completely forgot about where I came from, God, my problems, my loneliness, and people's judgment of me. I felt like I belonged. Our relationships weren't always perfect, but they were far better than any relationship I had ever had up to that point. In many ways, this was good for me. I was able to step outside of the prison I had created for myself, and I was becoming more extroverted. I was learning social skills that all those years of isolation and hatred had prevented me from learning. I was discovering how dating relationships worked. I was discovering girls, pornography, a new sense of autonomy from my parents, drugs, and a life apart from God. This was a Chase I had never known before.

The drugs for me happened much the same way they happened for my brother. I looked at the drugs as the way I could fit in with many of the people I was beginning to become friends with. They were doing them, so I just did them out of the necessity to fit in. It was weed and pills--the same as my brother when he started. My friends at work did not approve, but my friends at school did. In the beginning, they were incredibly fun for me. We would get high and forget about everything. We would laugh, do stupid stuff, drive around and try to get with girls. That was pretty much about it.

By the time I was seventeen, I had gotten into enough trouble that I decided to leave my parents' house. I was ready to go. I had a friend from school that just happened to live one neighborhood over from my parents' neighborhood. This friend tended to party hard and, now that I was living with him, I had to do the same.

This all might just seem fine on the surface, but people are like oceans. When you look at them, you can just see the surface of the waters; there is so much more underneath. Many times, the deeper you go, the darker the water gets and the stranger the creatures are that live there. During this time of working at the diner, hanging out with friends, going to school, using drugs and partying, my perspective began to change again. Once again, the way I saw the world was on the move. My perspective began to shift from exploring my new reality, and discovering new things about myself and other people to a creeping feeling of hopelessness. I had gained enough tools in this season to move on to the next, and look at it a different way. What I didn't know was that what I was trying to run away from was faster than me, and it began to catch up.

This new season was not a good season. Just like when spring comes, and things began to grow again, what I had planted the previous season was growing something that didn't look pretty. We don't always realize what we are planting in our lives until the next season when that seed sprouts. As soon as I moved out of my parents' house, I began to feel alone again, even though I was surrounded by people. The partying was not fun anymore because those feelings of helplessness came along with it. We would party or smoke weed just about every day, but there came a time when the partying could not sedate these things anymore. I could be drunk and sedated physically but my perspective was still warped; the feelings of helplessness and hopelessness would not go away. They were present even when I was intoxicated.

When I say my perspective was changing, I mean that how I saw things was changing. My perspective was becoming gray. Have you ever looked at one of those color tablets with the interchangeable plastic colors? You can look at one, move another tablet behind it and the color changes to whatever the mixture of those two colors create. Mine was a mixture of darkness (black) and light (white), which meant what I saw was now transforming into the color gray. I don't mean philosophically or ideologically gray, but I mean physically gray. The color and vibrancy of the world was being sapped from me. I saw everything through the lens of gray.

I have to note that, around this time, I met a young girl whom I began to date. She and I met at school and at the time, she just happened to fit the bill. We used drugs and partied together. She was looking for someone who would love her, I was looking for an escape, and somehow we fit together. We were not compatible mentally, socially, emotionally, or in any other way, but we each provided the other with what we needed at the time.

We dated from the middle of my junior year in high school until I was around twenty. She was looking for love and I was only able to give her crumbs of dysfunctional affection. Even though the relationship was unhealthy, I found an escape from myself in her, and, eventually, she got pregnant. I was nineteen at the time and so

Gospel Realities

obviously was well equipped emotionally and financially enough to provide for this new baby. No worries! Of course, I'm being sarcastic; I was a mess. When she told me the news, I ran off and tried to get as much cocaine as I could to run away from it. I honestly don't remember if I even succeeded in that mission or not. I felt like my life was crushed. I even tried to get her to abort the baby. She wouldn't do it. This baby was going to come, and I was going to be a father. Right in the middle of all my mess, my struggles, my attempts at escaping from myself, the drugs, and all the other mental and social dysfunction that that brings, I was going to be a father. In the midst of it all, my hopelessness and pain persisted and my gray outlook never abated. I realized, I wasn't going to be able to escape this time; I was living a new reality, whether I wanted to or not.

Chapter 4
Controlling What You Can't Control

We all have to step from one dimension of life to another. We don't always get to pick when, or how, or what motivates us to do so, just as we don't get to pick what family we are born into. The seasons of life change, and we have to learn to adapt, or we will be destroyed. We may not always like the next dimension of life that we are walking into, but we can see it from a distance. We know it is there, waiting for us, and we can either wave at it or try to run away from it, The conveyor belt of life continues to move us forward much faster than we can run in the opposite direction. No one is exempt from this. Only death separates us from this truth, and even then, we are thrust into a new reality.

Learning to adapt is an integral part of life. There are thousands of books on it. There are sermons, daytime talk shows, and websites that tell us how. Most of the time we can't tell how well someone is adapting to whatever season of life they are in until they can no longer adapt. This doesn't always have to be brought about by a new season; it can be a new job, a new family dynamic, or a new life challenge that is thrown your way.

Gospel Realities

Most of us try to adapt on our own. We try to take the reins of life and direct it to where we want it to go, but the more we try to steer it, the more it goes the way we don't want. We don't get to control everything. People will fight for control. They will kill, steal, and destroy just to get it and, when they do, they realize they don't really have it. That only makes them hold on that much tighter.

Maybe the truth is we were never meant to have control. The more we aim for it, the more we discover that those attempts just hurt us. What if I were to tell you that there was someone in control who can handle all of those things much better than you can? This notion makes some people angry because they view the one who has control as the one who is most valuable, the most important. It makes them feel helpless and less than because they don't.

No one likes to feel helpless, but what if I were to tell you that the one who has control wants to help you and has a far greater capacity to help you than you have to help yourself? We tend to hold very specific ideas that people who have control are evil dictators, harsh bosses, demanding governments, drunken angry fathers, and people who live in a state of disaster as they try to hold on to control for dear life.. What if I were to tell you that these negative images are generated because people were never meant to have control in the first place?

There is a God who "...sits above the circle of the earth, and its inhabitants are like grasshoppers...." (Isaiah 40:22). The Bible tells us that "The LORD has established his throne in the heavens, and

His kingdom rules over all" (Psalm 103:19) and "The LORD is in His holy temple; the Lord's throne is in heaven; his eyes see, his eyelids test the sons of men" (Psalm 11:4).

The Bible gives us a picture of a new reality. The Bible gives us a revelation of a holy God on a holy throne, who rules over all, and who cares about us. This relates to us because "The steps of a man are established by the Lord, when he delights in his way" (Psalm 37:23). A man's steps are not only established by God, but present us a new reality which assures us that "for those who love God, all things work together for good, for those that are called according to his purpose" (Romans 8:28). These Scriptures tell us that God is in control, and He helps establish the direction of our journey. If we love Him and are called according to His purpose, then this journey we are on is going to work out all right.

Those who fight for control are those who want a better outcome for themselves. Don't get me wrong. There is nothing wrong with wanting a good outcome for your life. That is natural and good, but trying to control every aspect of your life is harmful and destructive. A revelation of God's sovereignty does not just give us new information, but it also gives us permission to let go. So many people have been trying to hold on to some semblance of control of their life in their career, their spouse and children, and their precious reputations that they have lost sight of themselves. They live in constant stress over something they are fighting for but can never have.

Gospel Realities

Let's go back to Isaiah 40:22. Did you catch the fact that the Scriptures compare us to grasshoppers? No one likes to feel like a bug. A bug is small, seemingly insignificant, annoying, and easily squashed; no one wants to feel that way. We may not be bugs, but this verse says we are "like" grasshoppers compared to God's sovereignty. We hop around, fly around, and squirm around our lives looking for control, annoying everyone around us, laying eggs that produce more people fighting for control. All the while, we are trying to dodge life's attempts to squash us. The truth is, however, if we hang around the wrong people long enough, we will get squashed.

People often times fight for control because, without it, they feel insignificant. They feel helpless if they can't control it all. This desire may manifest itself in many different arenas in our lives. The desire to control doesn't stem from our situations, but from us. This has been present since the dawn of man. The Garden of Eden is a good illustration of that. God told Adam "…You may surely eat of every tree of the garden, but of the tree of the knowledge of good and evil you shall not eat, for in the day that you eat of it you shall surely die" (Genesis 2:16-17). Genesis goes on to tell us that the Devil, in the form of a snake, crept to the first woman Eve and caused her to doubt God's command. The serpent told her "…You will not surely die!" (Genesis 3:4) He convinced her that God had prohibited eating from the tree because He didn't want man to be like God. There was a battle for control already raging in the heavens and Satan wanted to bring that battle to earth. Satan wanted to create the same rebellious nature in the woman that he himself possessed. She partook of the fruit, gave it to the man, and sin and death entered the world. Thousands of years have passed since then, but the battle still rages on.

God has given us an alternative, though. He has given us permission and invited us to let go. That is what I couldn't grasp. All those years of trying to manage my pain only increased it until it overflowed from me and entered the lives of others around me. I did not have the ability to heal my own pain, nor did any counselor. We had tried and failed. That was a wound that only God could heal. My response to my pain was to run away—to run, dip, dodge, and dive to avoid it. I thought I was fast enough to outrun it, but the pain kept creeping up on me.

Without the understanding that there was a God in control, I kept trying to do His job. I didn't know that every time we try to do God's job, we wind up getting hurt. Many times, as a pastor, I try to do the job of the Holy Spirit. I have never succeeded. I cannot convict somebody, I cannot convert anybody, and I cannot produce lasting healthy transformation in someone's heart. I can only do what I am called to do, and that is to preach the gospel. I have no control over the effects of my message. My job as a pastor is to surrender to the power of the Holy Spirit in my preaching, counseling, as well as every other area of my life. If you try to do the Holy Spirit's job, you can turn into the stereotypical televangelist Reverend Deep Pockets

Gospel Realities

who will do anything for a following and pretty much anything for a dollar.

Have you ever wondered why people strive so hard for money? Realistically, we must work to eat. We must work to live. So money is important in that regard. It is also true that being successful or rich is okay. The problem occurs when money is elevated to a high position in the heart. What power does a green piece of paper have? What value does a gold coin have? Exactly. The only practical use I can think of for a green piece of paper is to throw it into a fire for a little bit of warmth or possibly toilet paper. Money gets its power from what it represents--security, influence, and the freedom to do what you want when you want. It represents the ability to sit back and breathe a sigh of relief knowing that if something bad happens, you have a security blanket that will provide for your needs. Do you see what all those things have in common? They all represent control. This is just one aspect, but on closer examination, you can discover how many different problems in our life revolve around this battle for control.

In the previous chapter, I related how my life had taken a very confusing, somewhat destructive turn. What I didn't divulge in is that God was beginning to work in my life in a very powerful way. He was beginning to leave clues in my life--evidence if you will--of the truth that was just out of my reach at the time. There was coming a point where that battle for control was going to reach a climax, just like the plot in any story, and there was going to be a resolution. For that to happen, I had to first get sick of fighting. I had to surrender. There had to come a surrender before there could be a victory.

As I explained before, my perspective was turning very gray. There were three fundamental occurrences during this period of my life where I collided with a different reality. These collisions eventually led me to the truth. There were three encounters with three different people that began to change the way I viewed God. The first one was seemingly insignificant. It happened while I was a cart pusher at Wal-Mart at the age of nineteen. I was out working when I ran into a stranger in the parking lot. He was a middle-aged black man that was one of the most joyful people I had ever met. I only encountered him briefly but he made an impact on me that will last a lifetime. I only met him walking in the door, but when I saw him, I saw this light that emanated off him.

Some people may describe something like this as an aura, but it was definitely something that I had never seen before. He also said three simple words that put that aura into perspective for me. He said, "God bless you." That's deep, I know. In that moment I knew that I knew that I knew that he was a Christian. It was a truth that was immediately placed onto the forefront on my mind that very moment. The best way to describe it was that I just knew it.

The second occurrence was similar, but at a different level. I was working at Chili's as a waiter, when the pastor of the church that I grew up in came in for lunch. He was with a group of people and I assumed they were having some type of board meeting. When they

Gospel Realities

came in and sat down, they sat in the section that I was covering. The same light was emanating off them, except this time it was so intense that I was scared of it. I did the best I could to serve his table while pretending not to know him.

The third time I saw this light, it was on a person that I will tell you about shortly. Before I get to him, I want to tell some of the back-story to put it into perspective for you. It was the same light that I had come to recognize as "Christian." I tell you all this because none of this happened while I was on drugs, or because of drugs, or in some intoxicated state, or because of any action of my own. These occurrences happened in my life because they were orchestrated by the same God who "…sits above the circle of the earth…" (Isaiah 40:22). They weren't just some sort of existential experience but were more like clues, or evidence--what the Bible calls "signs"(John 2:11). They were leading me, in the midst of my pain, to the One who was able to heal. They were signs pointing me, in the midst of the battle between darkness and light that left me in a state of gray, to the One who is the light, and helping me to understand that "…God is light; and in Him there is no darkness at all" (1 John 1:5). The darkness that was in me was the result of the absence of God in my life. The light I had seen on those people was no coincidence. John 1:4 says, "In Him was life, and the life was the light of men." What I had been witnessing was the light of God shining through these people.

God has a history of working this way. He likes to leave clues about Himself everywhere. He wants to tell us who He is. He wants to tell us where truth can be found. Our reality may be our reality, but it may not always be the truth. Jesus said, "I am the way, and the truth, and the life. No one comes to the Father except through me" (John 14:6). He wants to meet us right in the midst of everything that is happening in our lives and reveal to us who He is. We may be telling ourselves so many lies about ourselves that they seem like truth. Sometimes it takes someone outside of ourselves to reveal to us the source of the pain, the struggle, the sense of hopelessness, the lie that we can fix all our problems by ourselves, the belief that money will bring us a blanket of security, or that drugs can remove our problems for us. We aren't really looking for solutions. We are looking for a person, and we don't even realize it.

We are not looking for some new philosophy. We are not looking for a new crowd of people to take our minds off our problems. We are not looking for a simple release from our issues. Instead, we are desperately searching for someone to redeem us even in the face of our problems. We are looking for someone to give us back what has been stolen from us. Jesus comes to do just that. Our problems work together for our good, when God has called us, because they reveal the deep wounds within us. Our healing becomes so much more necessary and urgent, which takes us one step closer to the Healer. We look for answers, but what we really need is a relationship. An answer can solve one problem in our lives, but a new one will arise. An answer won't sustain us in the space between one problem and the next; instead, it sedates us only until we are swept away by the next issue that arises. A relationship with a person, on the other hand, sustains us and helps us to heal.

It is impossible to take steps towards such a relationship without a decision. Many of us are so jaded by life that we have to have a house fall on us. "Give me a sign," we say, believing that this sign will make our choice for us. The Bible could have used any other word, but God chose "sign" (John 2:11, 3:2, Matthew 24:3). A sign is something we see when we are on a journey. It gives us direction. A sign doesn't get us there, but it points the way. When you are on a journey and you are lost, one of the greatest things you can see is a sign. When you are lost you can feel hopeless and helpless, especially if you are alone. A sign is not a person, but signs usually point us to a place we can find a person. We can mark our life out by time and direction. That's how my navigation system works. You type in a destination, and it will give you directions and how long it will take to get there. We don't have one for life, but we have one for travel.

Each of us travel in life, though not necessarily geographically. We change jobs, family dynamics, cars, friends, churches, hobbies, as well as location from time to time. Perhaps there comes a time when we cannot pay our bills. This might be a sign that it is time to change jobs. If we are observant, we can see signs in our daily life—signs that indicate what our next move should be. Many of us spend a great deal of time trying to change the circumstances that surround us, but that cannot fix the deeper problem. We can change circumstances all we want and be as broken and alone as we ever were. That's because what needs to change is us. God began to reveal that to me by showing me glimpses of the light that He is.

My pain revealed my need for a physician, my hopelessness revealed how I was created for hope, my loneliness revealed my desire for a relationship, and my imagination revealed in me a desire to be in another world. All of these things lay dormant within me. I had no understanding of what my capabilities were. There was a solution though, and before too long, when the time was just right, I would find what, or better yet, who I was searching for.

The battle raging within me was nothing new. The nations of the world have been won and maintained by battles. There have always been rulers rise to power, whether they be chieftains, presidents, or kings. That has always been the case, and rulers have had a tendency to rise against each other to threaten or conquer a neighboring nation. This happens today. One of the best examples of all of this would be North Korea. You do not even have to do anything to stir up Kim Jong Un; you just have to be a leader of a world power and you are on his radar.

Since God made an earth to be ruled, there has been an attempt to conquer it. There has been a usurping of dominion, not by force, but God's choice in granting man the right to reign over the earth. When that first sin was committed, the shots were fired here as they had been in heaven already, and the battle began to be waged here. The devil is called the "...prince of the power of the air...." (Ephesians 2:2). He has been a prince for a while now, but he is not king. He has influence, but not supremacy. What do rulers fight over? They fight over territory. If a nation opposes another nation, it usually means there is going to be a shifting of territory.

The Old Testament prophet, Daniel, once prayed for help in a situation and God sent an angel to help him. The angel didn't make it to Daniel right away and Daniel waited for days. When the angel finally made his way to Daniel, he explained by saying his delay "The prince of the kingdom of Persia withstood me twenty-one days, but Michael, one of the chief princes, came to help me, for I was left there with the kings of Persia" (Daniel 10:13).

There is a king of heaven, and there are ones on earth. The earthly king reigns over one area. The heavenly reigns over both. The earthly king establishes his power, but the heavenly one reserves all rights to invade the other. Notice though what the angel calls the opposing demonic prince. He calls him the prince of the kingdom of Persia. There was a designation given to this demonic prince that associated him with a territory. This is how heavenly battles take place—in much the same way earthly ones do. The earthly ones merely reflect the heavenly ones, which came first.

The angel was opposed because he was entering a demon's established territory. Demons know well enough that when God sends an angel to do His bidding, it is a serious threat to them. Imagine what would happen if I marched over the border of North

Korea with an American flag strapped to my back and a machine gun in my hands. They would undoubtedly fire on me. The same thing is happening in this passage. The demon sees this angel entering his territory and attacks him. The demon might not have known why the angel was coming, but he didn't have to. He knew this angel was sent from God, and that was all he had to know to pick a fight.

This demon put up so much resistance that Michael, the archangel, the head angelic honcho, comes to support this angel. This must have been a sizeable threat. This angel had been fighting against this demon for three weeks. I don't think I could battle someone for three hours. Angelic beings do not have the same limitations that we have, though. This apparently was a sizeable, aggressive threat, but the purposes of God were so great, that the leader of all the angels was sent to aid in this mission. Ultimately, the angel emerged triumphant.

This battle has not stopped. It will continue to go on, and Christ will continue to reign, "...until he has put all enemies under His feet" (1 Corinthians 15:25). This is a battle where there is no break, there is no truce, nor will there ever be. There is no cease-fire and there is no surrender, until Christ reigns. The territory that is at stake is crucial. Christ has given man dominion over everything (Genesis 1:26). Territory is comprised of many elements. We may think of national borders, culture, and governments, and this is all true as they apply to the concept of territory, but the most important thing about territories is that they are made up of people, and with the people come the power. It is not the land that gives power to the territory; it is the people. So what role do people have in this battle?

Not a whole lot on their own, but there is something unique about people that thrusts them right into the middle of this battle. Man is made in the image of God (Genesis 1:26) and that makes man a crucial component in this battle. In ancient times, pagan gods were represented by images or idols. An idol was set up to act as a concrete version of an abstract god. Everything a pagan god could do would be done through this image. This gives us proper perspective for why man, being made in God's image, cannot be just an innocent bystander in this war, but is instead a target.

That's why me crossing the North Korean border with an American flag, (a sign of who I represent), and a machine gun (a sign of my intentions) would be so stupid. I would automatically be shot, no questions asked. None would need to be asked. That is why all people, Christian or not, are placed in the middle of this battle. Because we are all made in the image of God, we represent Him, whether we want to or not. We didn't ask for it. It may seem unfair and cruel, especially for the passive, but it is our reality. You may not believe me, but the Bible reveals the reality of this battle. Ephesians 6:12 says, "For our struggle is not against flesh and blood, but against the rulers, against the powers, against the world forces of this darkness, against the spiritual forces of wickedness in the heavenly places." I would admit, we won't always be able to see the battle, but we can see the side effects. If God's reality is true, then there is an eternity. That puts the battle into perspective then, because it becomes about so much more than just survival.

The apostle Paul describes those who believe in Christ as Lord and Savior and have died, as merely fallen asleep (1 Thessalonians 4:15). So, death in the context of this battle is not the physical death; that is merely sleep. The reality of death from a biblical perspective is much more severe.

The battle is about more than just survival or we would say they have "lost," they were "defeated," or their "service is finished." The battle is really about eternal destinies; it is about whether those on earth will spend their eternity in heaven or hell. Either way, it is clear we are going to live eternally somewhere. For those that already are Christians, it is about the battle for their faith, which affects their joy, their peace, and even their hope. For those that do not trust in Christ as their Savior, it becomes about preventing them from seeing the truth of the gospel. Paul the Apostle tells us in 2 Corinthians 4:4, "In their case the god of this world has blinded the minds of the unbelievers, to keep them from seeing the light of the gospel of the glory of Christ, who is the image of God."

How does he blind them? The god of this age (Satan) is very resourceful. He is able to mix up circumstances in our lives that cause us to become distracted from any sort of eternal reality. He allows some form of false teaching to plant itself in our minds to deceive us of the truth. He sedates us with pleasure or the allure of an easy life, and we then become sedated to anything of eternal significance in

Gospel Realities

our lives. He can make our lives hard enough that we get so caught up in fixing our circumstances--financial, relational, etc.—that we become merely a twenty-four hour on-call mechanic for our own lives. Whatever the situation may be, it can blind us from the truth of the gospel.

The apostle Paul, the man responsible for the writing of much of the New Testament, was the same way before he was healed of his spiritual and physical blindness. Paul was a Pharisee, a religious leader in the time of the early church. He thought belief in the Christ was a threat to Judaism, and so took upon himself the mission of persecuting the followers of Christ. Paul was doing his mission, and doing it well, when he had an encounter with the risen Christ himself on the road to Damascus:

> But Saul, still breathing threats and murder against the disciples of the Lord, went to the high priest, and asked him for letters to the synagogues at Damascus, so that if he found any belonging to the Way, both men and women, he might bring them bound to Jerusalem. Now as he went on his way, he approached Damascus, and suddenly a light from heaven shone around him; and falling to the ground, he heard a voice saying to him, "Saul, Saul, why are you persecuting Me?" And he said, "Who are You, Lord?" And He said, "I am Jesus whom you are persecuting, but rise and enter the city, and you will be told what you are to do." The men who were traveling with him stood speechless, hearing the voice but

seeing no one. Saul rose from the ground, and although his eyes were opened, he could see nothing. So they led him by the hand and brought him into Damascus. And for three days he was without sight, and neither ate nor drank. (Acts 9:1-9)

Saul was not only blind, but a persecutor. His hatred had developed so much for God and anyone associated with Him that he even held the coats of a mob that killed one the early followers of Jesus, Stephen, who became the first Christian martyr (Acts 7:58). He was blind to Christ, His message, and His followers until he encountered Christ for himself. When Saul encountered Christ, he encountered the same light that I described to you, just in a different way, and he encountered the voice of Christ. This wasn't a drug-induced state or the result of wishful thinking, but was a personal encounter—not to someone who was gullible or easily misguided, but a persecutor of the church and an educated man. Paul did not have a philosophical or ideological encounter because of a textbook in a classroom; he had a real, personal encounter with the risen Christ. Later, when a man named Ananias came to where the blind Saul was staying, he prayed for him and what looked like "scales" fell from his eyes. (Acts 9:10-19) We did not see the scales, but we saw the effects of his blindness. It took an encounter with God for Paul to "see" his own blindness, as well as the prayers and words of another, for the scales to fall off.

Gospel Realities

Chapter 5
The Night Gets Darker

When I found out that I was going to be a father, my perspective really began to shift. With this baby on the way, things began to come into focus for me. I realized now that my lifestyle of partying, wandering, and irresponsibility had to come to an end somehow, but I did not know how. I can still recall the emotional weight I felt. Now those feelings of hopelessness became mixed with feelings of stress and anxiety. I never had a child before, but I knew that there was a train coming down the tracks at me, and it wasn't going to stop and it was not going to slow down. It was just a matter of time before it hit me. My girlfriend was just as clueless as I was at the time. Neither of us knew what our next steps should be. She knew we had to schedule some doctor visits and some things here and there for the general well-being of the baby, but neither one of us were prepared to handle the lifestyle change, the mantle of responsibility, and the shift from selfishness to selflessness that a baby required.

It felt like we were just waiting for the train to hit us. The worst thing about this whole situation was that our lives were a total mess. We had in no way, shape, or form the resources to provide for even the basic care of this baby. On top of that, our relationship, especially after news of the coming baby, was growing more and more tense and dysfunctional. The stress of the train about to hit two kids put our nerves on edge. If you have ever had a child out of wedlock, you may relate to these feelings.

This is where the stereotypical role of a man in this situation would come in. Sensing the stress of the baby coming, this is the point that he would leave not only the relationship, but maybe even his zip code, in order to run away from this "problem." A baby, much like money, holds its power not in itself, but what it represents. Who could dislike a baby? Babies are cute, small and smooch-able. I know that not everyone would agree, but a lot of people would. A baby brings about a lifestyle change, a shift of perspective and priorities, and the ability to tough out sleepless nights. You have to deal with the looming reality that your life has now just had a steel cage put around it that limits what you can do, where you can go, and when you can do anything. The days of just getting a wild thought in your mind and going to the movies are over. That is incredibly scary for many, but this is the reality of a baby. Babies bring much joy, but they also bring much pain. You cannot separate one from the other.

If your life does not change in these ways, you are going to be a bad parent. The thing with being a bad parent is that it just doesn't just affect you. You don't just have to wear the social badge on you that says, "Hi my name is Jeff, and I am a bad parent." Your child has to grow up wearing a badge that says, "Hi my name is Stephanie, and I have bad parents." Not only do you and your child wear that badge, but your own parents wear that badge as well. It is the badge that says, "Hi my name is Bill, and I have a son who is a bad parent and I am ashamed to say so because that makes me look like I was one too." That would be a big badge to wear. I know but you get the point.

Suddenly I was hit with an ultimatum. Do I stay and wear a badgeless shirt, or do I leave and wear the badge? I am blessed to know that I chose the former. After the initial shock of the news, I was able to settle into this new reality. I was able to accept that this baby was coming, no matter what that entailed. The good news for my girlfriend and me was that those same loving parents who did the best they knew how for me had not changed in that regard. They were there and they were willing to help after the shockwaves had cleared, (my mom ran to the bathroom to throw up after I told her the news).

My parents knew I was being an idiot at the time, but also realized that my idiocy was not just going to affect me. It was also going to affect this baby. For the sake of the baby, they agreed to help us pay for an apartment that was pretty decent, to say the least, for my girlfriend, myself, and the new baby to move into. They were covering the essentials for us. They wanted us to have a suitable home for the baby when she came. Our relationship had been dysfunctional before, but with the added stress and changes that were required that neither of us really wanted nor were equipped to engage at this point, our relationship grew even more tense.

Gospel Realities

The arguing and fights really got out of hand. My life was beginning to feel more and more hopeless. The drugs had not stopped; my usage actually increased. Now it was no longer just weed and whatever pills we could get at the time; cocaine and ecstasy were in the mix. The emotional trauma of a new baby coming, immaturity, and drug use was a recipe for disaster. That train that was coming down the tracks to hit us felt like it was not just going to hit us but it was going to wreck and make our lives train wrecks too. The very thought of it made our lives a living train wreck. You see, my perspective was getting darker and darker as more "darkness" settled into my life. The people that I was hanging with were becoming darker and darker, and so much so that it scared me. Some were capable of just about anything and even gave me a really eerie feeling to be around them. I was so far gone from that child I once was. I was choosing this darkness over all that I had known before. The thing was, I was getting so used to this darkness that I didn't even recognize it anymore. It had become my new permanent reality.

What had caused me so much trauma growing up—my brother's drug use and my lack of attention because of it—I had now become. I was now nineteen, the same age my brother had been, and doing the same drugs that he had been doing. I was living in the same darkness, and feeling much the same way he had been at that time. I had a kid out of wedlock, I was a drug addict, my parents had to help support me, and I was in an incredibly dysfunctional relationship that brought me nothing but pain. This was my new reality. This was the

The Night Gets Darker

world I had chosen. At the cusp of what was supposed to be me stepping into a big opportunistic world, I was groveling at the bottom of it. I smoked cigarettes at this time, and I remember going outside to smoke just to get a moment of solitude, wondering to myself when all of this would be over.

I wanted to be out of this, for it to be over, but only a hopeless prediction of my future set over me. There is a pain that is created by a bad circumstance, but there is another pain that hopelessness creates, one that is not dependent on a circumstance, but cuts deeper and with surgical precision down to the very heart of man. It is a pain that no pill can cover up, that sleep will not get rid of, that does not come in waves, but floats over you and inside of you. It is a weight landing heavily onto your chest; with no one around you to help pick it up, it slowly crushes you.

Despite all this, I had left those former co-workers behind for the time being. I had not heard much from them nor had I attempted much to reach them. I again felt isolated. I felt like their world, their reality, was not mine. Their reality was much better, much more lighthearted than the one I was living. They had made smarter decisions, and they were not drowning. The worst part was that I thought they were better than me and that I was a pity case. When I was around them, I felt even worse about myself, if that was possible. I could not stand feeling that way, so I separated myself from them. In the middle of this entire thing, the baby was coming. My little

Gospel Realities

Sophia was born on September 24, 2009, and my life was slowly beginning to change.

The darkness that I felt was not a result of a chemical imbalance or the result of a series of bad days. This "darkness" that I speak about is the side effect of a battle. Colossians 1:13 says for those that have put their trust in Christ, "He has delivered us from the domain of darkness and transferred us to the kingdom of His beloved son." I was living in this dark kingdom. The kingdom that I was living in, this territory, did not belong to God but was dominated by a different kind of ruler. My perspective was dark and growing darker the more that hopelessness crept into my heart. The more I ran to drugs, the more hopelessness would creep in. They only revealed to me the disparity of my situation. This was not a metaphorical darkness, but a real darkness. If we watch a movie that is really violent and gory, we would call it a "dark" movie, but this is the type of darkness that takes its place inside of a person. It sets up its throne in someone and influences every decision that he or she makes.

There was a fierce battle raging that affected my circumstances, my perspective, and my soul. How could I be so arrogant as to say I am so important that heaven and hell would wage a war for me? Well, on my own, I'm not. The fact is I am made in the image of God and that makes me important (Genesis 1:26). An attack against me was and is an attack against God. The Devil was stirring any circumstance, highlighting every insecurity, pouring hopelessness

The Night Gets Darker

over me so that I was so drenched with it. All I could think about was getting dry. I was looking so intensely at these problems that I was missing the solution. I was looking so aggressively at myself and the people around me, that I did not look at the One who wanted to transfer me into the kingdom of Christ (Colossians 1:13). The churning machine of hopelessness was so loud in my mind that I could not hear the bullets flying over me. There was a battle raging for my soul and, before anything was to get better, it had to get worse. Jesus had to die before there was a resurrection. Those who came to Him had to be sick to be healed. There has to be rain before a rainbow, and there had to be a battle before there was a victory.

I was blind to the gospel. I had some incredible experiences with people carrying the light but the time was not yet here for me to see what that really meant. When someone has a gunshot wound, he is not thinking, "what is for lunch?" He is thinking of the pain. In the same way, my pain was so great that I could not see. The scales were still on my eyes. They had been on for a long time, but the time was just about to come when they would fall off. I had these encounters with the light and I had people praying for me. The dynamite was in place; it was just a matter of pressing the little red button.

Gospel Realities

Chapter 6
No Way Out

In antiquity any city that had any significance was surrounded by walls. It had to have a line of defense to hold off the enemy or prevent an army from just marching up and getting in. In the same way, we as people build walls to prevent anyone from getting inside, where our heart, our emotions, and our thoughts are located. Depending on how vulnerable we feel, we may build bigger walls. We not only build the walls thicker so no one can get through, but we also build the walls higher so no one can climb over. We wait on top of these walls, with our words and our attitudes, and shoot arrows at anyone who approaches them. We have the capability of building a pretty significant defense system.

We build the walls and then we build a very narrow gate to get in and out of our walls. It would take someone incredibly special for us to want to come out through that gate. After all, anyone could try to lure us out and assassinate us! What we don't realize is that, while it keeps others out, it also keeps us trapped in. No one else gets in, but we are stuck inside. If we stay inside those walls enough and never leave to go the fields outside for food, we will wither away. We will never be the person that we could be. We really build these walls because we have had a history of people invading. They have come in before and ransacked us and so we are not going to let that happen again! We build walls for other people, but those same walls keep God out. With those walls up, we cannot become the person He desires for us to be.

The Bible says, "For the kingdom of God is not a matter of eating and drinking but of righteousness and peace and joy in the Holy Spirit" (Romans 14:7). It is not physical food that we are looking for, but righteousness, joy, and peace. God wants us to open that little gate for His Son to feed us what we really are craving. Righteousness is the first thing in that verse. That is merely a way of saying what we are fulfilling our end of a relationship. It is merely opening the gate to Jesus in our lives. The joy and peace are what come to you as a side effect of letting Him in. We all look for deep-seated joy and peace in our lives. I am not talking about the kind that comes and goes depending on circumstances, but the kind that can be present no matter if we are in paradise or hell in our lives. If that is not true of you, all you have to do is open the gate. Even if you are already a follower of Christ, you just have to keep the gate open.

God demands of us our very lives and everything that makes us belongs to Him. He calls us to hand it over. He calls us to give up our lives as He gave up His for us. Matthew 16:24 says, "Then Jesus told his disciples, 'If anyone would come after me, let him deny himself and take up his cross and follow me." Everything that God would have us crucify, He replaces with the things that are central to

His kingdom—righteousness, joy, and peace (Romans 14:17). He says himself He will. "Give, and it will be given to you. Good measure, pressed down, shaken together, running over, will be put into your lap. For with the measure you use it will be measured back to you" (Luke 6:38). You will not find this type of giving and receiving alone. There is no trade in a market made of one man.

Much of the reason I suffered so much was because of the walls I built. They were walls built because of insecurity that became higher and thicker. The more hopeless I became, the more walls had to be built. The thicker and higher my walls, the safer I felt, but the darker I became. What I didn't realize was that the invaders were not coming from the outside, but from the inside. Walls don't protect much from an assassin when he is working with a spy on the inside….and that spy is you.

Gospel Realities

Chapter 7

Back to Square One

My daughter Sophia's birth did not change everything right away, but it definitely made the need for change more urgent. As I continued to do drugs and party from time to time, I was reminded that this was not right. This was not the lifestyle a good father was supposed to have. It began to gnaw on me. At this point drugs had no longer were a fun recreation for me anymore, but a burden that dragged me down. I was not an addict in the sense that I needed them to get me through the day, but I was an addict in the sense that when the vortex of hopelessness began to open up in me again, the drugs were a release to escape that.

Weed was not capable of sedating me and my growing burden. Cocaine was able to do it temporarily. I would buy some from whatever shady character I could, then do as much as I could in order to get away from myself. I had to do more and more, not because of chemical dependence, but because of a wound that just seemed to hurt and bleed more. I had to push the limits of what I knew I could handle. Some days I would wonder if this would be it. I wanted to push the limits enough to fall off the edge and into the abyss of death. I did not know what that would hold for me, but I did not think about it either.

There was a battle of thoughts in my mind at the time. My wounds called out to me, but so did the notion of being a good father. I wanted to be a good father; I just did not have the ability to be that person. The weight of all this could not be carried in an immature, dysfunctional, and unstable relationship. The relationship with Sophia's mother eventually ended abruptly and my mother came and picked me up from my apartment. I do not know when or why I even called my parents, but they were there shortly after the final fight. I cried in the back seat of their car on the way to their house. It was around nine at night, and my life could not go on like this anymore. I was traveling back to the place where the pain began. The pain of the past seemed like such a distant memory by that time. The memories driving that pain had dissipated or I had managed to force myself to forget them. Either way, whatever pain was there belonged somewhere in the past. The pain I knew now had become just pain, detached from any memories, detached from my childhood, and it just ran its own course.

I was returning to where I began. My parents didn't say much on that ride home. It was as if I was being swept back into their arms as a child again. This time, it was not because I bumped my head or was tired, but because I had adult problems. Walking into my parent's house this time felt like a blanket of security wrapped around me. I felt safe, and this place really felt like home. My parent's home that once felt like a prison block for me now was a paradise compared to the party houses, and drug houses filled with shady strangers where cigarette smoked floated above your head. This home had a warmth, a vibrancy about it. It felt like home. There was a feeling of possibility in the air.

That first night felt like sleeping in a bunker for a night after months and months of tireless fighting on the front lines. The next morning, I got up for breakfast and my parents were already at the kitchen table eating breakfast, which was their normal Saturday morning tradition. I went to the table feeling a little shell-shocked, a little ashamed, and not knowing what I would do now. We spoke for a little while and my mom asked me a question that I believe shocked her even as she asked it. She asked me if I wanted to move back home.

It was a strange question to think about at the time. I had made such a rebellious show of leaving and never planned to come back, but after the hell I had been through the last three years, it seemed like all those memories didn't even hold a place in my mind anymore. There was no feeling of resistance anymore, and there was no animosity. There was no more rebellious teenage anger. There was actually a release, knowing that I could stay at a place that felt like this. I had gotten used to living in cold dark homes, where you never know what was going to happen next. Because of my upbringing of being raised in a stable home, even though I had been anything but stable in my teenage years, I had never felt at home in any of those

Gospel Realities

environments. To my own joy and surprise, I responded with a big "Yes!" My parents agreed. They laid out a few ground rules for the home and that was that. The next chapter was beginning in my life and it would be totally different from what had come before. I was once again stepping into a new reality.

I had to adapt to live at my parents' house. Amazingly, it presented no difficulty at all. I no longer wanted drugs. I was so sick of them by the time I got there that I was happy to leave them behind, as well as everyone who was associated with them. I know it doesn't happen with everyone like this, but they never really held much of a chemical grip on me, just an emotional one. Now that I was being exposed to some new constructive emotions, I easily laid them aside. There was no need to run away from my feelings anymore. I had to get a job now and I had to figure out what I was going to do about my daughter. She had stayed with her mom at the apartment, and I had to see her.

I applied at a local temp agency and, after a short while they were able to get me a steady, decent paying job at a manufacturing plant within five minutes of my new home. My mom also helped me by directing me to and going with me to see a lawyer in town. This lawyer had known my family and had helped with the plethora of my older brother's speeding tickets in the past. One could write an entirely new book on his driving alone. He helped me set up a parenting contract and I received joint custody of my daughter. We had established a schedule to have the child on certain holidays, and I would get to see her every weekend. A place of stability had finally been developed in my life and now this reality I was entering was much nicer and more secure. I felt like I would finally be able to take my life back.

Gospel Realities

Chapter 8
Home Sweet Home

There is something really unique about home. We all wake up there, we get ready for the day there, we have to leave it for a while, and we usually want to go back there when we get off work. It is our place of solace, and it is a place where we know we can kick back and release the tension of whatever the day has thrown at us. It is a place where we can have people over or seclude ourselves if we want. It is a habitat of joy if we have good relationships with those with whom we share that home, or it is a place of misery to avoid if those relationships are bad. If we have a good home—"home" being a relative term—it is a place that we look forward to going to. I say it is relative because we can live in a shack, apartment, or mansion and all of those can still feel like home.

It is almost as if we were built for home. We may not all be homebodies, but in some way or another we will really struggle if we do not have a home. We do not truly feel at home when we are on the go, but we have to be stationary to live somewhere. It is a place we go to, not go with. This is not something that we have to ask science or philosophy to know we feel this way; we just know it. I would propose that this feeling just doesn't come on its own.

Gospel Realities

We were meant to feel this way. We were meant to look forward to home. You can move all around from house to house and each one of those places can be home because this principle is always at work within us. The Bible says that those who have trusted Christ have been called with an "upward call" (Philippians 3:14). When God calls us, He calls us to Himself and His home. God has made us to desire a home, because He wants to call us to His. His home incorporates all the best parts of our homes now without any of the negatives.

God's home He has prepared for us is in a city (Revelation 21:10). It has more room than you could ever think what to do with (Revelation 21:16). It is more secure than any house with its defenses (Revelation 21:17), and is more luxurious than any city we can find on the earth now (Revelation 21). He does not just give us a city, but for those that Jesus has called, He prepares for us our own living space within that city (John 14:3). He has prepared it and God has made it so God Himself who is unseeable now will be in plain sight, and He will live with us (Ezekiel 37:27).

Much could be said about the New Jerusalem, the heavenly city God has prepared for us, but we have to know that that desire within us serves a much larger purpose. The people you connect with most are the people you would have over to your home. That will be true there too. The desire for home you have now is because you were not built just to find a home here. Actually, we realize the home that we are called to know will make us feel like "...strangers and exiles on the earth..." (Hebrews 11:13). It is a good thing to know that, as much as your home feels like home now, it really only serves as a sign or indicator that you were made for such a greater home, where every fiber of your being tells you you belong. This home you now live in is temporary, but this heavenly city will be one built for us for eternity.

This is again another sign that what we have here is just a foreshadowing of something so much more that is available to us. That desire I had to be in another world just stirred up in me something God had put in me. It stirred up in me something, but it did not tell me where. People look to other planets in the hope to colonize them one day. That is the pursuit of a home. There are people moving from city to city constantly hoping to find a place they can really call home. We have real estate agents that help us in securing just the right home for us and our desires. We are looking for a home. A home is much like money; it has no power in itself, but its power resides in what it represents. A home represents all the good things we were designed for. A home is about who is on the inside. If you have a beautiful mansion but live with a cold and distant wife than that is far from a home. If you live in a shack and work as a mechanic, but have a wonderful, loving, and supportive wife to come home to, now that is a home.

Home is about so much more than the American materialistic ideal. For those called with that "upward calling," it is a city that every part of us is made for. God is the one who will make this place

Gospel Realities

like home. There will be others there, too, and they will add to the splendor, but the source of everything that makes that city majestic is God. We can look for a home, but we aren't always looking for God. We want the things we were made for because we are made in His image. We don't want to give Him credit for these desires that are within us. We may not even realize that we should give Him the credit for it. Our desire for a home is a mere reflection of our desire for a true, eternal home.

Chapter 9
Uncertainty and the Presence of God

I don't know how I perceived my future at that point in my life. I was twenty years old, and a single dad working full time. I did not know where I was heading, nor did I have much time to think about it, but I did know that at least my feet were on solid ground for the time being and I was headed in the right direction.

One day the idea to go to college just hit me. I had no idea what I even wanted to do. I suppose merely going to school to provide a means for myself and my daughter was a good goal for the time. I remember back in high school I had tossed around the idea of going to school for marketing and trying to enter that industry, but that was mainly because I thought in some way that it would be a glamorous profession. I would move to New York and be rich. That was about as far as I got with that vision.

I also tossed around the idea of becoming a marine. At the time I was considering this I felt pretty lost and hopeless, like I had no skills, and no real ambitions for the future so the Marine Corps looked like a way to develop some skills and give me some time to think about what my future might look like. Both these ideas were

Gospel Realities

just wild ideas. I had almost gone through with the Marine Corps idea, but because of my lack of follow through, I did not pursue it. Looking back, it was for the best, in my case.

I looked up the local community college and applied there. I had no particular interest in any type of degree. I figured a business degree was basic enough to get my foot in the door a lot of places, so I started there. To be honest, I really was just toying with the idea of going to college. In the back of my mind I thought I would just apply to college, try for a little bit and fail. It was just a random shot in the dark for me that I didn't expect to really take me anywhere; even so, it seemed like a positive step in the right direction, so that is what I did.

By this time, I had reconnected with one of my old friends from that diner where I had previously worked. We had both grown a lot since then. Okay, maybe not in maturity, but the seasons of life had taken us to a different place since high school. We both had one thing in common we liked to do, and that was party. Most weekends I would head up to his place after work, usually after midnight, to party. That was a crazy time to try to join a party. It was almost one a.m. by the time I got to his apartment and showing up at a party at that time meant that a lot of people were already drunk. I remember walking into some crazy scenes sometimes. There is no need to get into details, but you probably get the idea.

At that time my life consisted of work from four p.m. to midnight, and then partying all night on Friday or Saturday night.

Uncertainty and the Presence of God

Eventually I switched to a day shift where work ended right at four p.m. I would get off work, go to a night class, come home, party on Friday or Saturday night all night, and then come home and be a single dad on the weekends. Those times were incredibly busy to say the least. If it was not for the foundation I had at my parents' house, I would not have been able to do it. They were supportive of this new direction I was taking, so they let me live there for free and save up some money when I could.

I was so sick of the former lifestyle I had that I wanted to leave that behind. I wanted to forget about the darkness of that person I once knew. Staying busy helped me to forget about that. I began to search for a new identity and a new reality. I developed a lot of confidence in myself during that time. It was not all healthy. I worked out fairly hard then, so I tried to find some identity in working out and bodybuilding. I also began to think of myself as quite superior to many people. It was like living a double life. I had this side of me that was a single parent, which carried with that all the dark memories of the past and all those failures, and there was a successful positive side to me now too. There was a battle of identity there as I stepped from one reality into another. I was becoming popular with people that would have rejected the old me, and I felt superior to those that knew the Chase from those dark times.

Where was this heading? It felt like my past was trying to drag me down, but my future was changing and calling me forward. I did not see the hand of God in any of this, and for the most part

Gospel Realities

God never entered my mind. I was so caught up in finding out who I was and pressing forward into this new identity that my life became very self-centered, other than my time with my daughter, and even that was slightly tainted.

My brother's life was changing too. Not for the better though. My brother, due to a series of affairs and that nagging drug problem he still had, was about to be divorced. His life had continued to prosper at work, for he was a very successful sales representative for a very successful company, but his family life was diminishing. He was a hero at work, but a zero at home. Many can relate to this story, especially in the United States. This devastated my brother. He was in much the same conundrum that I had been in. He had a wife and two daughters and wanted the best for them. He really did and still does. He just did not have the power to do what was needed to give them the best. He was stuck on himself, much like I was.

Due to our similar upbringings, we knew what a healthy family looked like. We were never perfect, obviously, but he knew the relationship our parents had and knew you really could have a marriage that was beneficial, rewarding, and full of love. He knew it was possible, but he did not know what they had put into that relationship to get there. He knew that my parents had almost divorced for selfish reasons shortly after they were married. He even knew that it was God who miraculously spoke to each one of them during their separation and led them back to one another. That encounter had led to their surrender to Christ in their lives, which

Uncertainty and the Presence of God

created a legacy that we were and are still becoming a part of. He knew all this, but he had not tasted it for himself.

He was distraught over the possibility of divorce. He knew he did not want it, but he also knew that he did not have the power within himself to reconcile this relationship. During this time at work, he was transferred to another location in our city where he met a man named Dave, who was a Christian. He was not the Christian who just wore the Christian "badge", popped into church every now and then, and hoped for heaven one day because of his good deeds. He was a Christian who knew God on a personal level and in an intimate way, and who carries the light of Jesus within him to this day. He did not just give lip service to being a Christian, but lived out what he said. He shared Jesus with my brother. He counseled Bret even in his current situation to give his life over to Jesus, no matter what his problems were, and to let God intervene in all his mess.

That is obviously a big request to make of somebody. To give, not just a weekend here or there and a few dollars, but your life, is a big request. My brothers and I grew up in church, and we understood what this meant. It was no small commitment. Giving up your life means giving up your attempt to control it, your autonomy to do whatever enters your heart or your mind, and to surrender to the losing battle that you have been fighting to win. It means handing over your values, your selfish priorities, and even your own idea of what your future will hold. It was not a surrender that he was willing to make right away. He had to dip his foot in the water first before he would dive in.

He attended Dave's church, and sat in the back. Many reading this have been there before. You know the sights, the sounds, and the feeling of not just sitting, but living in the back row. Moving up rows is a scary thought. You might be noticed. Association many times means social accountability. The back row does not make such high demands. So, for the time being, the back row it was. He dipped his foot in, found that the water was suitable, and decided to dive in. He gave his life over to Christ, and eventually recommitted himself to Him.

I had no idea all of this was going on in his life. I knew some stuff was going on. I knew he was having marital problems, but I had no idea the magnitude of everything that was happening. Once again, I was sheltered, not by force, but by my own self-centeredness. I was so caught up in my life I did not even notice what was happening in his.

I did not know until after all this what my brother thought about me. We had done drugs together off and on before this, so my brother was hesitant to share what had happened to him. He felt like a hypocrite. I could imagine. He felt he couldn't just come up to me and say, "I know we used to do drugs together a few months ago, but I met Jesus, and my life is totally different now." After hearing about the pipe dreams that many drug addicts have to fix their lives, one

Uncertainty and the Presence of God

more can feel like an exhausting waste of breath. I can see why he would have thought that.

We had a conversation once during this period. I do not remember about what exactly. Maybe it was him attempting to share this with me. I remember looking up at him and seeing this light on his face, and there was something in his eyes that I had never seen. This was not something I could put my finger on, so I just had to take it at face value. There was a look of vibrancy in his eyes, a look of transformation, and if you could describe it, there was a look of new life in his eyes. There it was, that light again. Several times I had seen this light, but I always just pushed it to the back burner of my mind. It sounds pretty stupid, doesn't it? It sounds stupid that I can see all this that cannot be explained by science or reason, and mere words cannot give it justice. It was in a book, but one I thought had no relevance in my life. Due to my own blindness, I would not even let it register as something worth investigating further.

I was later invited to my brother's recommitment ceremony. I had not thought about God in a long time. He was very far from my mind, but I was about to enter a place where He was at the center of many people's lives. I was about to go to church. I woke one seemingly regular Sunday morning. Whether I had partied the night before or not, I do not remember. I got ready and headed an hour away to this church Bret had been attending.

We walked through the door and, immediately, into a mix of people. There were black people, white people, and hispanic people.

Gospel Realities

They were smiling and talking with one another. I came in the door yawning and the associate pastor of this church greeted me at the door. He introduced himself and asked if I wanted a cup of coffee. He pointed me to the coffee and I was shocked by the gesture of kindness. What was this place? I had been in church hundreds of times before, but I was seeing this church with new eyes. Little did I know Bret had been sharing with his Christian friends how he wished he could reach me but felt like a hypocrite for even trying. I am sure this pastor was aware of this. Do you remember the light I have been telling you about? This whole place was filled with it. Not the building itself, but in countless people. They were all filled with this light. Once again, it did not affect me.

We made our way to the front row of the sanctuary. This was not my choice. My parents led me there. I had no idea what was going on. I should have known the ritual, but I had not been to church in so long that I forgot. We stood together as a group and sang some songs. The lyrics were on a screen in front of me and not many were professionals in there, so what was there to lose? I sang now because I wanted to be nice. I was on the front row, for all to see. I sang just to be polite.

There was a pool that they had brought into this dimly lit sanctuary for baptisms. "Let's do some baptisms or whatever," I thought. There was quite a lineup for that morning, so Bret was not the first to go. Each time a person got into the water, the pastor would ask them a few questions and give them the opportunity to

Uncertainty and the Presence of God

share some of their story as to why they were doing what they were doing. I remember listening as each person shared a story of how God had brought his or her family together. Each of them had problems and dysfunctions in life, and God had reconciled what would have otherwise been irreconcilable. I remember hearing story after story, weeping the whole time. I was fighting back tears as much as I could, but they kept coming. I was so moved by these stories, yet I had no idea who these people were. Looking back, I know that what they had is what I wanted so desperately in my little family, but I felt powerless to attain it.

My brother's turn finally came. He followed suit behind the others. He shared his testimony, much of which I had been pretty much oblivious to. I was moved to tears by his story, as well. I could not let anybody see this, obviously, so I fought hard to keep it back, but it was like there was no turning the hose off. Bret was baptized and when he came out of the water, he shouted and gave Dave a big hug. This was definitely something that had made an impact on Bret. It was beginning to have an impact on me, as well.

Next came the preaching. It had been so long since I had heard a sermon, it was like a figment of my distant past. I listened though. I do not remember a word the pastor said that morning, but it moved me once again. I didn't cry, but his words stirred my mind and I was beginning to register what he was saying in my heart. I could only shake my head from side to side as he preached because what he was saying was somehow reaching inside me. It was like

Gospel Realities

being hit from the inside, and it stirred everything I had come to know. The room was lit up with an atmosphere like I had never seen. It was as though I could feel the heart of someone much bigger than me all over the room. What was going on here moved in a way that drugs never had. This experience reached, not just my body, but something deep inside of me that made me physically react. The atmosphere was tangible, but not in a physical sense. It was there if you could see it. Otherwise, it just looked like a room with nice lights. This was more than just lighting effects; there was evidence of a personal intelligence in the room. This intelligence was not only present, but was reaching inside of me to reveal to me something that I had never tasted or seen before.

Chapter 10

The Only Way Out

There are turn-around moments in many people's lives--countless stories of great leaders who experienced one moment that redirected the course of their lives. In some ways, this seemed to be such a moment for me. In many circumstances where someone has an epiphany it gives him new direction for his life and that is pretty much it. The experience will spark some new wave of creative energy that will help the person to invent, to strategize, or to revolutionize a market somehow. This was not that kind of epiphany, though on the outside it could look like that.

  One danger you can run into when sharing your testimony is that it can give people the wrong impression, especially with those outside the faith, depending on how you word it. I do not want to give you the impression that this moment was merely an epiphany or that the circumstances of my life just began to fall into place from that moment. All the things that happened after this moment were not an effect of my circumstances changing. That wasn't even my goal anymore. They happened because I changed.

  In that moment, I was confronted with a reality that I had not been able to grasp before. I had not only heard and seen this new reality; but I had tasted it. When we taste something, we see it, we

Gospel Realities

grab it, and we put it in our mouths to get an idea of what it is really made of and whether it has any real quality. This I tasted. This new reality had made its way inside of me. This reality was not a new set of circumstances, or a new goal—though that became part of it—but it was the reality that this God is real. He is not just real, but He is "real" involved. He is no longer just some concept to be discussed or some idea to hate, and He had just revealed Himself to me. The days of running away and rejecting Him were over. Now I had to make sense of something that had never made sense.

Either I had to deny everything I had previously thought I knew about God, close my eyes, plug my ears and run, or I had to accept the fact that what just happened actually happened. I finally took in Who I had run away from for so long. I think my oblivious nature towards all of this was really a blessing. Someone whose nature is to study and examine everything that comes his way would have had to study this, examine it to see if it fit his paradigm, and discard it. There is nothing wrong with that, if you assume everything about your paradigm is correct. This was something totally new.

This was not just an experience for me that happened and that I could leave in the past. This was an experience that turned on something inside of me. There was a switch that had lain dormant in me that had flipped. There was a button that needed to be pressed, and it was pressed. The very essence of life was deposited into me then. It was not the essence of physical life, though the Bible does say that "In the beginning God created the heavens and the earth"

The Only Way Out

(Genesis 1:1), and God "created mankind in his own image" (Genesis 1:27). This was the very essence that gave life to my physical body. My once dormant heart towards God woke up. It was suddenly sensitive to Him. I was instantly aware of what of He approved of and was moved to follow those things. The Bible said this very thing would happen. The Bible calls an experience like this being "born again" (John 3:7). This new heart He gave me was part of this new birth. The Bible speaks of this new heart in Ezekiel 36:26, "And I will give you a new heart, and a new spirit I will put within you. And I will remove the heart of stone from your flesh and give you a heart of flesh. And I will put my Spirit within you and cause you to walk in my statutes and be careful to obey my rules."

When you are born, you come as a package. You come with a mind, a heart, a mouth, ears, eyes, a nervous system, and other things that help you function. Some of these things can become distorted because of the effects of sin entering the world, but they come to help you function. They are part of what makes you the person you are. Ezekiel 36:26 said He will first give you a new heart. He will give you a heart that is moved by Him. It is a heart sensitive to the very presence of God Himself. He will give you a heart that is full of life, vibrancy, and moved by things that move God. After spending so much time fighting to shut myself off, to build walls, and remain insensitive to God and anything else, my heart had become stone. In a minute, God removed that heart in a spiritual sense and gave me one that is capable of such things.

Gospel Realities

He not only performs this heart transplant in you, but He pours His Holy Spirit within you. This Spirit is the same Spirit that was there in the very beginning of God's creation. It was the same Spirit that was "...hovering over the face of the waters" (Genesis 1:2). The Spirit that was there in the beginning of all physical creation is present and active in the beginning of a man's spiritual creation. Whenever God creates something or does something magnificent like this in a person, His Spirit is always there. His Spirit is God Himself. He does not remain estranged from what He does on earth, but He is present, doing the very transforming work in a man that only He can do.

Our birth is the start of a new life. As I write this book, my wife Tara and I are waiting very expectantly, and not always patiently, to have our third child (time for a quick fast-forward in the story). When he is born, this will be his physical birth. He will come as a package deal, just as the rest of us do. He will come with all the specific faculties that come with a healthy child.

He will not be born again, but born for the first time. He will not come with a new heart, but a natural one. He will come with a set of dormant and active desires that oppose the very God who births a person again. Our son will break the very commandments given by the God who created the heavens and the Earth. In doing so, he will fall short of the beauty and majesty and honor that he is required to live up to in order to live in perfect harmony with God (Romans 3:23). He will be alive, fresh, new, beautiful, and a good creation of

The Only Way Out

God, but he will be spiritually dead in his "trespasses and sins" (Ephesians 2:1). He can be a healthy, beautiful, crying baby, but he will be born a spiritual stillborn. He will be dead to the very essence of life itself because of his sin and will have to be born again, just like anyone else, to receive this life beyond life, this empowering, this enduring, this vibrant new life.

This sounds morbid I know, but it only sounds morbid to those that are used to this type of death. This "sin" sounds like too much; it seems too heavy a condemnation to those who are used to sinning. This life seems too good to be real, like it is something that maybe only Hollywood can think up. It seems detached from the reality we are prone to. Those that are used to being alive and dead at the same time would think this. This reality seems impossible to us because we don't know the God who makes this happen. When we think like this, we think like men are used to thinking and what comes natural for us. That is what Matthew was speaking of when he wrote, "Jesus looked at them and said, 'With man this is impossible, but with God all things are possible" (Matthew 19:26).

There is a reality that we are not used to. There is a reality we long for but don't know how to get. Science fiction movies depict alternate worlds. Romantic comedies depict a reality where everyone is laid back, a little funny, and true love is found. Action movies need a hero to step in and save the day and set everything right again. There are books that create fanciful love stories. Worlds with warring magical elves and other mythical creatures that capture and invigorate

Gospel Realities

our desire for a new reality that is greater than ours. These capture us because we imagine ourselves in them. We sit back and observe this alternate reality from the safety of our living room sofa. We long for this new reality, so we spend hours immersing ourselves in it, sometimes to the detriment of the reality we really do live in. We long to be a different version of ourselves in a different reality where we can shine. We spend much time crafting our social media to shine, whether we really think this about ourselves or not.

I assure you this is good. This is what we are wired for, though it is often misdirected in harmful ways. We were created to live in a reality that is not this one. We were created to live in a reality much better than the ones we read or watch movies about. Those are only shadows of a much greater reality we are invited to step into. We were created to live in "…a new heaven and a new earth…" (Revelation 21:1). We were created to shine here in a much greater way than all these movies and novels can even touch on. We were created to "shine like the sun in the kingdom of [our] Father…" (Matthew 13:43). You will shine like the sun, not because you are the hero who came in and saved the day, but because "…God so loved the world, that He gave his only Son, that whoever believes in Him should not perish but have eternal life" (John 3:16).

Everything about a normal reality outside of God has become normal for you because that is what you have settled with. The movie, The Matrix,[3] captures this very well. Neo the central character played by Keanu Reeves lives a seemingly normal life. He works a

The Only Way Out

decent white-collar job and everything is pleasant for him. He even helps his landlady take out the garbage. All the while, something inside of him longs for more. He spends his nights searching his computer for clues that would lead him to this greater reality.

He meets a character, Morpheus, that tells him that what he soon discovers is not the truth, but merely the tip of the iceberg of what is really out there. He is offered the chance to see the truth if he takes a pill. One pill awakens him to the truth of reality, and the other one lets him forget the encounter and wake up to what he has come to know as his reality. He chooses the pill that takes him further. He wakes up shortly after this experience to a new world, one where he wakes up in a body size vat, in a huge factory of sorts, that contains other giant vats with people still stuck in a reality that is impressed upon them from the outside. It is a reality that deceives them from knowing the truth. Neo wakes up and removes from his body the cords that have kept him alive while being he was being incubated in this vat. He has been distracted just enough in this false reality, the Matrix, to keep him occupied and settling for something false but satisfied enough to get him to stay. In order for Neo to know the truth he had to be born again.

He was going through the motions of an everyday existence but something within him called out for more. He was looking, but he did not know what for. He just knew there had to be more. Neo woke up to a world that was on the brink of destruction. It was lacking resources, and mankind was about to be conquered by a race of machines. Neo was mankind's last hope at stopping this invasion. Neo takes on a Christ-like persona to save the human race by sacrificing himself in order to restore all mankind to the place they were when they had dominion over the earth, and so others can wake up to the truth.

We create stories that reach out for the truth of who we are. We create what has been wired within us. This movie would not be labeled a "Christian" movie, but it illustrates the dormant knowledge in us that we were made for something more. We were made for more than just survival of the human species. We were made for more than just success at work. We were made for a life of truth, a life of deep meaningful relationships, and a life of thriving and not just surviving. We were made for more than what we have settled for. There is a greater reality, and it is calling out to us.

We immerse ourselves in these worlds because that is what we were created for. We spend so much time on Facebook, checking our likes and managing our online persona. We want "likes" at the cost of a few meaningful relationships. We look for a community. We thrive in one. Facebook has harnessed this fact about our human nature, and it has done it well. We have settled for the superficial approval of people we barely know, just so it makes us look on the outside like we are thriving, while deep down we know the shallowness of those online relationships. We settle for the feeling it gives, even though we know it is superficial, instead of pursuing real meaningful relationships. We can be in a room full of people, but still be on our phones, totally disconnected from those around us, looking for the superficial. We try to avoid the profound need for real relationships that are not being fulfilled. God knew we would need this type of intimacy when He created us. He offers us a relationship with Him so intimate that He doesn't just like us on Facebook, but He is willing to make His home within us (John 14:23).

He wants to create in us the place where we long to be, where we will thrive. He wants to make His home in us. He does not just want to check in every now and then, eat our groceries, and forget to clean the toilet seat. He wants to share a meal with us, spend time with us. He wants to live within us. He wants to be with us while you spend time with others. All those things that bring us closer to another, He wants to do with us.

We can be in a room full of people and still feel alone. We can be in a sexual relationship with someone, physically connected, while being emotionally and socially estranged. God desires so intimate a relationship with us that every longing we have for real meaningful relationship is found in Him. He desires that for our own good. As a result of our relationship with Him, all of our other relationships fall into their proper perspective.

All those relationships that need to be reconciled, He wants to reconcile. All those relationships that are hurting you or are keeping you from your destiny, He wants to remove. He wants to heal what is hurting, restore what is broken, sharpen what is dull, and

Gospel Realities

bring beauty to what is marred by sin. After all, Jesus was a carpenter, and that's what carpenters do. They shape and mold raw materials into beautiful, usable things. Shaping wood is one thing that takes talent, but His real desire is to make us someone more beautiful than what we could have ever imagined. He wants to beautify what life, sin, hurts, and failures have marred in you. He was beginning to do that in my life; He can and will do the same for you.

Chapter 11

A New Perspective

When this new relationship with God began to form in me, I wasn't conscious of it, but it still took root. This new life that had just been sparked had not been forced, but it had been received. I struggle to find words to illustrate this grace, this gift that was given to me despite everything that I had done to deserve otherwise. I can call it a gift because it was not a burden. It was not some new philosophy or self-help program. It was not something that tickles your imagination for a while and then leaves you to acclimate back to the real world. This was a gift that did not even stay in that room. This new life that was sparked in me was one that I carried out of that room, and back to the reality that I had come to know. I was heading back to the same set of circumstances as before. I was still a single dad working full time and going to school. My reality was still the same on the outside, but now this reality of new hope had been placed in me.

    I began to see everything through the lens of this new promise that God was birthing in me. I was going back to the same job, but the way I viewed my job was completely different now. I actually cared about how I did my job. Before I was just working to get a paycheck, and apparently had rubbed a few co-workers the

Gospel Realities

wrong way but I was too oblivious to really even know it. I cared about the people, I cared about the way I did my job, I cared about sticking to these commands that were now in my heart, and I cared about providing for my daughter and me. Before that Sunday, all I cared about was providing for my daughter and just doing what I knew I had to.

Some might claim, "Okay, now he subscribed to Christianity, so he did what he had to do to follow the program and get social acceptance." This is not true. To be honest, I had not read the Bible in years besides occasionally when I was around fifteen and did not really understand much about it. I knew the Bible stories like Moses parting the Red Sea. I knew some stuff about Abraham. I knew Sodom and Gomorrah got nuked by God, and Lot's wife turned into salt because she looked back. Maybe I remember that because of the intense pictures in the children's storybook Bibles. Either way, I did not know what I was getting into. I hadn't read much of the Bible, and I would not know what to subscribe to even if I had wanted to.

All I know is that Who I experienced in that room that day was real. It had made a major impact on me, and it was one that I could not and did not want to shake off. I felt this magnetic pull in me to read the Bible. I don't even know if anyone ever told me I was supposed to. At least I do not remember being told. I did not read it to avoid feeling guilty. I just knew that I knew that the God I met that day was the God in this Bible. I wanted to know more about Him, and I knew the Bible was a book I could go to everyday to do

A New Perspective

that. I had this overwhelming compulsion to pray. I wanted to talk to this God. I wanted to connect with this God. The same presence I felt in that room that day was the same presence calling out in me to do these things, except that now it was inside of me.

I had the stirring within me to connect with others about this same God. Once I had learned enough to articulate the Gospel, the story that makes all this possible, I wanted to share this too. I also felt great pain and great joy in doing this. I admit that, as I learned more about this God, that part of me that still struggled from the past wanted to manipulate all that I was learning and harness it for selfish reasons. I also didn't automatically live all those commands out right. I still considered some things okay that were really sins. I knew enough to get started, but I was learning just enough to become dangerous to myself.

There was still a part of me that wanted to measure up. When my brother started using drugs and I lost the attention of my parents, I began seeking it from everyone else. I felt affirmation from people when I got their attention. I was looking for a way to measure up in their eyes. I believed that the more attention I could get, the more I would finally reach this imaginary goal of measuring up. I didn't understand that this was impossible. There is no mountaintop to reach. You can walk through the valleys and hike to the base camp. You can climb higher until you reach the ridge of this mountain, just to find a descent into another valley. You press on hoping to find the peak of this mountain, but you just keep discovering more to climb.

Gospel Realities

It is endless. It is exhausting. There is no map and you are always lost, climbing, but not reaching. The only view you see is a glimpse of the elevation you are at for a minute, but then the realization hits you that you are not at the summit yet, so you are forced to keep climbing. This is how it was for me as I tried to so hard to reach this imaginary goal of approval.

All that pain did not go away overnight. It was still there, lurking under the guise of religion. I worked harder to measure up, but now I called it a mission or evangelism. I called it whatever I wanted to call it, but it was still pain manifesting itself in ugly ways. I knew the pain very well. It had traveled with me for a long time. It had not left yet. I just put it in my pack with me. I would drive myself insane trying to ponder what God wanted out of me. I would feel the pain lurking beneath and thought, if I could do enough of what God wanted me to do, I could be healed of the pain, or at least numbed to it. Many people think Christianity is all about being positive, but the truth is we are still people who carry pain and baggage. We have access to the One who can heal us of it, but we still try to carry it a lot of times, just like everyone else.

Chapter 12

Baby Steps

I have no problem with titles, at least to a certain extent. Being called a Christian is okay. Sometimes it can give others that do not know what the reality of this relationship is all about the wrong idea, though. When we give circumstances, situations, or people titles, a stigma comes with it. For instance, when your boss creates a committee at work what comes to mind? You think meetings, boardrooms, leadership, decision-making, or something along those lines. What do you think when your boss has created a team? You might now think of cooperation, competitiveness, moving together, energy. Titles carry a connotation, whether negative or positive.

Christianity can do the same thing. You can call it that and it can carry the stigma of some program with it. Depending on your background with Christianity, certain images may arise in your head as well. For the longest time, the word "God" meant not measuring up to me. It meant ostracization. It meant disapproval. Explaining to people what I believe in, what I value, or the experiences I have with God can be a tedious task sometimes. There is a place for that, but sometimes, especially in casual conversation, it is just easier to say I am a Christian. Think grocery store conversation. No one is trying to discuss the meaning of life while standing in the checkout line. It is more like "Hello," "How ya' doing?", and "Goodbye." When you call yourself a Christian, you call yourself something that can carry a deep stigma with it.

According to the New Testament records, Christians were first called Christians (Acts 11:26) in a city named Antioch, which is near present day Turkey. Before this, they were called "believers of the way." They had to be defined as something. It made sense that the followers of Christ would be called Christians, so it stuck. This is the name's historical precedent, but since then there has been a lot of history to fill in the gaps.

You may say you are a Christian and some will think, "Crusades." Others, "anti-science." Others will think hypocrites and some others will think republican. That is just what fits the bill nowadays. Christianity has made an impact on culture. That impact sits well with some, and with others, not so much. There comes a point where you just have to get over all that and just claim your Christianity. You must be willing to deal with the consequences of what you are associating yourself with.

The more I shared my faith, the more I realized how different people are in their relationships with Jesus. I once hated Him. He stood for everything that hurt me. Now this life had been given to me, and I had picked up and moved to the other side of the tracks. I could not really articulate it, but the movers had come to my house,

Baby Steps

loaded up the truck and moved my furniture, so here I was, representing the God I had once hated.

Some love Jesus, some are apathetic, some are aloof, some hate Him, and some think He is merely irrelevant. Usually it is a mixture of some of these. Everyone has something to say about Him. You can usually tell just how a person views Jesus, not just by the words they say about Him, but by the emotion, or lack thereof, that accompanies it. I was able to see now, in just a matter of a moment, where I now stood compared to where others stood. All the hate that I had expressed towards Him, I now saw on some people's faces. All that love I was experiencing in Him, I got to witness other faces as well. Some had been completely transformed in a moment like me, and others have had a rocky relationship with Him. Like I said, people were all over the scale on the subject of Jesus.

I don't want to leave you with the impression that Jesus is just about making your life better. There are plenty of self-help books out there that can teach you principles for that, and a lot of them would probably help you. Though the Bible is, in a sense, a self-help book, it is not about helping merely your circumstances, but helping YOU, from the inside out. My encounter with God was not the absolute fix, but I would be lying to you if I said my circumstances did not get better. The way I saw everything changed because I saw God and myself differently. Now I had something I had been reaching out for for so long. So, of course, my circumstances

Gospel Realities

changed because the way I worked, fathered, and engaged in relationships changed.

I was doing my job much better now. I related to other people much better. I was starting to be respected in peoples' eyes. That had never really been the case before. I had always just felt like a face in a crowd, like no one that had any significance, but now that I had changed, people saw me differently. I was developing new relationships, and I was doing much better at school. My grades were now average, instead of barely passing. That sounds funny, but I had been getting by with near-failing grades in school for a long time; average was a definite improvement! I kept attending that church and people that I felt never would have talked to me, were talking to me and we were developing relationships. People who made salaries that I could not dream of making were actually asking how I was doing, checking in on me, and showing concern for me.

I was so used to dysfunction and detachment with people that this was really shocking me. Before the day I encountered God, I thought anyone with an ounce of success outside of my family would pay me no attention, and that I was just someone to be passed over. I had no idea how this was happening from my old perspective. This new reality that was inside of me resounded in me that all of this was because of Jesus. In some way or another, these people had encountered this same God, and He is what connected us. I felt a connection with them that I had never experienced before. I did not drink or get high with these people. I did not even do these people

Baby Steps

any favors, except now they looked at me and I could see love and joy in their eyes.

You might find it hard to believe that you can see something abstract like that in a person's eyes. Matthew 6:22 says, "The eye is the lamp of the body. So, if your eye is healthy, your whole body will be full of light." The Bible says this is true and that when you look in someone's eyes, you can tell a lot about him or her. You may see a light, or you may see darkness. If you look at someone's eyes as he is laughing, you can see what is coming out of him. If you have ever looked in the eyes of someone who is angry, or ever stared into the eyes of someone who is desperate, you can read that also. When I looked at these people, I saw light, joy, and hope. That is a lot to see in someone's eyes.

I was dating someone new whom I had met at school. For the sake of not putting anyone on the spot, I'll call her "Betty." Betty and I had an interesting relationship. We met at school and dated for a while. Before my encounter with God, we got along fine, and we had fun together. After my encounter, we still got along, but I began to change. The way I wanted to spend my time and my money was changing, as were my friends. My conversations with Betty changed, as well. When something like this happens to you, you just have to talk about it. I would talk to her all the time about God. There was an acknowledgment of it, a decency she had towards Him, and she would even attend church with me. She was nice about it, but she wasn't totally gripped by this Jesus. She did not share the same

Gospel Realities

passion as I did about Him. When you cannot share the biggest thing about your life with someone, you drift apart. I sensed God leading me away from that relationship and eventually we broke up.

That was one of many sacrifices I had to make. In the beginning, I lost all those I had considered friends. We had partied together, occasionally worked out together, and spent some time on the weekends together, but literally overnight I did not hear from them again. It was instantaneous. I never even told them I was a Christian or anything before it happened. They were just gone one day. That left me feeling very alone. On top of what was a demanding schedule and being a single dad, and with all these changes, I felt very, very alone. I was not alone, but I felt it, and it was real to me.

I had gone from being a person that hated God and being indifferent to someone who loved Him and represented Him. I also carried the consequences of associating with Him. I really felt like I was living out the command Jesus gave to "...take up his cross and follow me" (Matthew 16:24). Every day, I was living out a life of sacrifice for Him. Though some of these experiences were painful, I could not deny this new reality within me. It kept me pressing on. It was God who kept me moving forward. I felt alone because many of the people that used to hang around me were disappearing, but God felt so incredibly close. He was there every day, and as I learned to sacrifice for Him, He felt even closer. It was not a sadistic type of punishment, but He was removing everything that kept me from getting closer to Him. The Bible says that God is a jealous God (Exodus 34:14). He is not jealous like clingy girlfriend jealous, but the type of jealous that wants the very best for you and is willing to go to any lengths to make that happen for you.

My biggest problem had always revolved around people. It always does. It stems from how we see God, but it manifests in our relationships with people. I was always doing things to gain attention or approval from people in the past, but now they were leaving. Now it was just Him and I. I had to work out some things with God before the people issues would get resolved. I remember that when people left me, God stuck closer to me than a brother (Proverbs 18:24). We talked together, and we shared every moment of the day together. I would think about Him all day, then I would come home and read the Bible and do some sort of Bible study or read a Christian book. This is probably the point where many would point the finger and label me, "fanatic." That also carries a stigma with it. Think car bombs and sacred prayer shawls. I wasn't fanatical. I was becoming gripped in my heart, allured by His presence, and my intellectual dimensions were being expanded. I was learning what love is from God. I was learning Who it was who was always with me. I was learning what it would be like to be accepted, not because I measured up in someone's eyes, but because Christ measured up for me.

It was a beautiful and painful time. The pain cleared the way for God's healing. It was not until people were removed that I could

Gospel Realities

find out what approval really meant. I had to be taken out of the warzone to be stitched up. I was alone, but in better company than ever before. These moments were fundamental to the way I see God. They were the beginning of much more pain and much more beauty to come. The sacrifices I had to make with my relationships were ones that were only for my own good.

Chapter 13
The Doctrine of Reality

There is a bizarre thing going on in the world of theology. There is another battle raging. There is the battle of doctrine versus experience. There are Christians who say experience is the best indicator of truth in their lives, and there are Christians that say doctrine alone is the only way to know truth. There is also the tendency in the world of theology to pit them against one another. This is a terrible mistake that stems from a terrible misunderstanding.

There are those that say only the Bible can be relevant in a person's life, and there are those who talk as if experience is the true acid test for the truth. The same principle is at work in those outside of faith in Christ, as well. There are those that believe and rely on philosophy, abstract thought, and personal experience to determine what is truth, and there are those that say only science can be depended on. They say that only that which can be tested and proven with the scientific method in a lab should be considered truth.

Then there is the middle ground. There are those that say philosophy, abstract thought, history, and science can come together to find truth. There are Christians that say doctrine and experience are how we discover truth. The reality is that the truth is found in the middle. Science believers cannot rely on science alone to determine what is truth without incorporating other realms of study. Christians can rely on doctrine, and true doctrine makes its way into our experience. This is not always a cut and dry rule though.

A Christian should be able to say what the Bible says should happen, really does happen in his or her life. If you surrender your life to Christ, there really should be transformation that happens. There should be evidence that both doctrine and experience are colliding together in a romance that creates the offspring of transformation in your life. This is what I hoped to show you in this book. The middle is where I want to reveal my story. When we limit Christ to a doctrine, we miss Christ. That thinking minimizes Christ to just another philosophy or self-help method. Christ was a real person, and still is. He is not just another person, but He is the Son of God (Luke 1:35, Matthew 8:29, John 20:31). The doctrines about God are not God Himself, and God is not a book, but the Bible reveals who God is. Jesus said this Himself, "You search the Scriptures because you think that in them you have eternal life; and it is they that bear witness about me" (John 5:39).

If the Scriptures are what tell us about Christ, then that breaks down some misconceptions about who God is. That means that, as Christians, we do not pray to a book, we do not worship a book, and we do not bow the knee to a book. Christ is not words on a page but a reigning king. If He lives and moves freely, as He does in the scriptures, then He is a God that we can feel, taste, hear, and know. We should see evidence of Him in our lives. God is one that does not like to sneak in and out of someone's life. He likes to leave evidence of Himself all around. He does not do it by accident; He is purposeful. He wants us to discover it.

The evidence that He leaves may take us in different directions much like evidence in a crime scene can lead investigators to different conclusions, but the evidence God leaves always leads to Himself. When God revealed this light to me in the faces of people, it was not just so I could have an experience and write about it later, but so it would lead me to Him. He loves us and desires for us to know Him.

Gospel Realities

Chapter 14

Learning to Run

I was around twenty-two and God was on the move again in my life. I was beginning to settle on the fact that I was on the other side of the tracks now. God had radically re-oriented me and set me in another direction. It was an awesome new journey that was not a course that I dreaded, but one that brought me great joy. I was beginning to understand what it meant to be His disciple. I was beginning to discover who He was, even though I was just barely touching the tip of the iceberg. Now that we had established this relationship and I spent some time discovering who He was, He wanted to take me to the next dimension.

It happened at another service at the same church I had been attending since my brother's rededication service. We were worshipping during service, when suddenly an elder of the church came up to me and said to me words I will never forget: "God told me to tell you that you have gifts that you are not using." That was deep, right? It was simple, yet profound. I had no idea what he was talking about, so I just took it all in. I was not offended or upset but just wondered what that meant. I didn't think I had any gifts or anything that I had not used yet. I just felt like a "bro" that now knew God. I tucked that one away for a while in my mind.

It was not until about a year later that God began to readdress that idea. It was after another year of spending time in the Bible daily, praying, worshipping, sacrificing, working, going to school and being a single dad. It was another year of transformation in my life. It was another year in the crucible, though a joyful one. Out of nowhere, I had this new epiphany—if you will—about what God wanted me to be. It was a gradual but new train of thoughts, desires, and feelings in my spirit. There was something God was calling me to. God was calling me to the pastorate.

This was new, but it wasn't. When I was a kid, my great grandma used to tell me that one day I was going to grow up to be a pastor. Everyone just pondered that statement and took it in. There is something about the mark of a pastor that God places on a person that others can notice. She noticed it. This was just a back burner thought for a while, and when I started getting into trouble, no one was saying it anymore. The evidence of such a calling was just not there then, but things were different now. I was different, and people were noticing. I had returned to the God that I once knew.

I shared this with my pastor at the time. I wondered if I really was receiving a specific calling from God about this. My pastor told me that a calling from God has a passion, a purpose, and a peace about it. I had the passion for it. It was constantly on my mind, and my heart was continuing to be drawn to it. I had found a purpose in it. I had this overwhelming sense that this is what I was designed for. There was no peace about it, though. One essential element was missing. So I prayed about it. God spoke clearly to me about it. He said, "Your peace is knowing that I am with you." Well, I took that as a pretty obvious reply from God. Peace would not be found in the nature of the job itself, but in God, who would be with me all the time. This was a settling thing to hear. Knowing that God is close to you in ministry is of upmost importance. Sometimes, when you are walking in God's will, everybody else will leave you, but God will not. Even if He feels distant, just knowing that He really isn't creates a peace in you through faith that it is going to be okay, and that it is going to work together for good (Romans 8:28).

This next season of my life was to be a season of transition. I had to transition from my view of my future to God's view of it. A lot of my future was still uncertain to me. These last few years had just been seasons of taking a few steps and hoping they panned out. Now, the direction I was walking had to be re-oriented so that the steps I would continue to take would be unique steps that brought Jesus and I even closer. I first, had to hit a wall though.

The last few years of working full time, going to school part time, and volunteering in church ministries paid some dividends both financially, directionally, and spiritually, but they were not going to get me to where God wanted me to be as a pastor. I was only going to school part time, and it was going to take me eight or nine years to finish my degree. For those that have gone to college, you know that would be incredibly daunting and certainly draining. I had to work to support my daughter and I had to go to school to prepare for my future. There is nothing wrong with not attending college, but this was just the plan that God had for me.

My father suggested that we figure up about how long school would take if I quit my job and went to school full-time. My dad is a bank examiner, so he knows a thing or two about numbers and watching them play out over long periods of time. We found out that it would save more money in the long run to just quit my job and go to school full time, and it would bring the goal of finishing school that much closer to completion.

I really loved my job. It was a good paying job and the people there were like family. I had learned so much about God during those three and a half years of working at the manufacturing plant. The job gave me lots of alone time and was not very mentally taxing, so I was able to spend a lot of time thinking and praying. It felt like God and I would just work together for hours there each day. It really was a time of growth for me and my relationship with God.

Now there had to be another change. Once I knew for sure what God's next direction was for me, I put in my two weeks' there and enrolled at a local Bible college. That was another journey of discovering where God would have me go. When I went to enroll at this school, there was that light again, on almost every face. It was on the professors and on the students. I remember thinking shortly after I started there that this must be a little taste of what heaven is like since it seemed like all the people I was seeing every day were the people of God too.

They were full of joy and were very kind. Many of them just came up to me and started talking, even though they didn't know me. My classes were taught by Christian professors who shared the same passion and love for Jesus that I had. The school was beautiful and clean. The people were smiling and every class I went to I encountered God. It really was a beautiful place and time. I learned a lot in that school. The first week I went there, I was asked if I was a Calvinist. I had never even heard of that before. Soon, I learned the Scriptures and their meaning, the meaning behind them, the history, and who wrote them, and through God's Spirit, they really worked their way into my heart as well.

I would not have changed anything about that experience. I learned a lot about people too. I discovered some wonderful followers of Christ, and I discovered some that were not quite so easy to get along with. There were many that seemed like they would roam the halls just looking for a debate. Don't get me wrong, I like a good debate, but I do not have the emotional resources to go and search it out every day. That type of thing is not just something unique to Christians either. Have you ever known anybody who, no matter what you are doing, where you are, or what time it is, cannot help but talk about politics? Not just talk though, debate. It was kind of like that, except with theology.

Gospel Realities

During this time, I learned that a lot of Christians tend to hide behind theology. They hide behind doctrine while their character stinks. I have met Christians who automatically want to separate themselves into camps based on some particular belief. I even met some that will do nothing but bash you in the name of Jesus over anything in you they disagree with. I have also met Christians who will love you unselfishly, who will give you the shirt off their backs, and who will encourage and support you just for being alive. I once had a Greek professor (a particularly difficult class), who helped us arrange a study period outside of class and even paid for dinner for all of us in the study group. There were probably seven or eight of us in the class! Now that is loving if I say so myself!

During the summers, when I was out of school, I had to find a job. The first summer job I had I was a furniture mover. A classmate at school got me the job. Apparently, there were not a lot of people lined up to be movers. The job of a mover is incredibly physically demanding. It was grueling work, especially in those long, hot summer hours. We would meet at a cave where the shop was located, drive to a location in the city, load furniture, drive to a second location in the city, and unload the furniture where the customer wanted it. There were a lot of rich people who had a lot of furniture and who wanted to hire movers to move it. Not everyone was rich, but movers aren't cheap and rich people usually had more furniture to move.

Learning to Run

Some days I would come home from that job with white sweat stains on my clothes. I would come home completely drained, sore, and my tendons hurt every single day. I would be sore one day, get some sleep, get up and go do it all over again while still sore from the previous day. The hardest part was the people though. I will change names for privacy's sake. There was a man, Saul, who really didn't like me. Actually, it was beyond dislike; it was outright hatred. Even though I had not said much to him, he already had it out for me from the first week. I quickly discovered it was because he was not only an atheist, but he absolutely hated Christians who stood for their faith. He would constantly belittle me, call me names, and cuss at me. That was just his automatic disposition towards me. I actually did my job really well; he just made an effort to go out of his way to ridicule me in any way he could. He had a friend at work that would do the same thing, just not to the extent that he did. Saul was the ringleader.

He was about six feet tall and one hundred eighty pounds and his friend, Caiphas, was a six-foot-five or so, two hundred and fifty pound dude. He actually got shot nine times where he lived before. He showed me the bullet holes on his skin. It was pretty intense. This just might look like a case of bullying on the outside, but behind all that, there was spiritual warfare going on. Do you remember that battle I was telling you about earlier? Well, this is how it can manifest itself sometimes. The battle can come from people, circumstances, or from any number of things.

Gospel Realities

Satan can use people to do his will. God will use people to do His will. When God uses people, it brings joy and peace and takes those walking it out to a new dimension of knowing God. Those that are following Satan's promptings do it either consciously or, most likely, unconsciously, but it will bring pain, stress, tensions, and persecution to those living in God's will. Satan has opposed God for a long time, and still does through people. This can be seen in the realm of politics and popular culture, among other arenas. Satan opposes God's will, no matter what form that takes on.

Here I was, a Christian, seemingly alone, in this spiritual hotbed. There were many days where I wanted to punch Saul in the face, but I knew if I did, I would pollute the image of Jesus he was supposed to see in me. I wanted to retaliate, but I knew I was commanded to love him. He caused a lot of stress in my life that summer, but this process was good for me. When Satan attacks, he wants the Christian to back away from God. He wants you to get hopeless, remain hopeless, and turn away from Him. If you keep pursuing God and you do not shrink back, then you will win every time--guaranteed. So, I kept pursuing God and, day after day, I would be crucified through this abuse. It was good because I was learning not to let others' opinions of me influence or distract me. I was learning the cost of being a follower of Christ. I was learning how God wins a battle.

I kept pursuing God and it got to the point where I was praying and reading the Scriptures constantly. One Scripture that gave me encouragement was James 1:2-4, which says, "Count it all joy, my brothers, when you meet trials of various kinds, for you know that the testing of your faith produces steadfastness. And let steadfastness have its full effect, that you may be perfect and complete, lacking in nothing."

That verse was a reminder for me that persecution is to be expected, and that it is not some strange thing that is happening. It also reminded me that this affliction is not being wasted. It was producing character in me that will last for eternity.

Near the end of this season, I was really seeking God about it. God knew it hurt me so much, but God also knew what He was doing, and it was not out of his sphere of control. I continued to pray and I eventually discovered the key to overcoming in this battle. I began to say to myself that every time he curses me, I am going to bless him. The verse that inspired me to do this was Romans 12:14, which says, "Bless those who persecute you, bless and do not curse them." What a backwards way of thinking compared to what our culture teaches us to do in those situations! I was going to do it anyway. I made the conscious decision to do that. The next time I went into work, both Saul and Caiphas had quit their jobs overnight! They just quit and I never ran into them again. I think God was trying to teach me something.

The second summer job as a landscaper was much less physically demanding. I say that with much sarcasm. The job was again full of long, hot days. This time the climate of the job was

Gospel Realities

different. The physical climate was the same, but the spiritual climate was different. I was just a peon landscaper. I did grunt work. There was a lot of shoveling, hauling dirt and debris, trimming trees and bushes, and yard cleanup. There was a young man there named Peter. Again, name change. He was a wild young country boy. He said things first, then thought about them later, or not at all. I really liked the kid though.

We would have long talks during our days. We were usually sent to job locations together, so we would spend many days together working. He would ask me about God all the time. He even made the comment one time just out of the blue: "I think God sent you here to get me to turn back to Him." Talk about ironic.

Let's back this up a little bit. I spent many years trying to measure up in people's eyes. When I came to God, I tried to do the same. One way I tried to do this was through evangelism. I felt if enough people came to Christ through my efforts, then I would finally measure up. The problem with my dysfunction is that no one ever gave their lives to Him when I shared the gospel. I mean never. We would do street evangelism sometimes in Bible College and we would see incredible miracles. I mean the crippled would walk and all types of stuff. That was cool, but I never did evangelism for that. I just wanted people to give their lives to Jesus. It never happened, though. It felt like the heavens just shut on that.

My dysfunction was so bad that I started to despair over it. I felt like I was doing nothing, and I wanted God to just take me home. It was really bad. I even wrote my feelings out on my computer. It was so depressing I later deleted it. Through a series of dreams another person and myself had, God told me to turn my attention to intimacy with Him. He of course did not mean sexual intimacy, but intimacy in the sense of familiarity and closeness with Him. I was to pursue that instead of evangelism. That sounds heretical, but you will see what I mean.

So, this Peter and I continued to talk. I shared story after story with him about my testimony and showed him things about God from the Scriptures. He was like me, in the sense that he had a religious background but did not know much about God. He had even served as an altar boy in the Catholic Church as a child. Jesus was new to him, though. I had never seen God give me opportunities like this before to share the gospel. This is exactly what I wanted, and it was just handed to me on a silver platter. I knew I shouldn't focus on making Peter a convert but on continuing to develop intimacy with God in everything. It was about sharing those activities of the day with Him, just like at the manufacturing plant. Peter later decided to give his life to Christ. We prayed together, and he even said that he felt weird in his chest as soon as we finished praying. I will explain that later. One Scripture that put all of this that had happened to me into perspective was John 15:5 which says, "I am the vine; you are the branches. Whoever abides in me and I in him, he it is that bears much fruit, for apart from me you can do nothing." I abided and He provided. I had the idea of ministry all wrong. It was quite different from what I thought it would be.

Chapter 15
Relearning Intimacy

The first thing you might have thought of when I said the word "intimacy" was sex. This proves your fallen nature. I say that jokingly, but that is what my friend (codename Peter) thought when I spoke to him about this concept of having intimacy with God. Anyone who has ever had sex knows you can have sex without intimacy. You can perform the act but feel devoid of emotional attachment and joy in it. You may have experienced this if you have ever had a one-night stand. Such encounters leave you empty and alone. This is sex without intimacy.

I am talking about intimacy for the sake of intimacy. Healthy sex is between a man and a woman where there is first intimacy and then sex. There has to be emotional engagement coupled with commitment before there can be a healthy sex life. It was designed to merely be an illustration of the closeness between Christ and the church. That is why sex is designed to exist within the biblical commitment of marriage. Since marriage is designed to illustrate the relationship between Christ and the Church (Ephesians 5:32), sex, then, demonstrates that the commitment, or better yet, the covenant that is already in place.

Gospel Realities

Most of the problems associated with sex in our culture revolve around the lack of this element. When faithfulness has been broken, then there are problems. When a husband cheats on his wife, there are problems. When a boyfriend has sex with someone besides his girlfriend, that creates problems. Yes, this even applies in relationships where no one is a Christian. When two men have sex, this creates medical and emotional rifts that we were not designed for. Children are created from sex and, without a commitment, this creates lack of harmony between parents. Believe me...I know that first hand. You might be in a relationship where sex is involved, and you are only dating. Sex is fun, but in the back of your mind, you do not truly know if that person will be with you six months from now. The longer you merely date, the more that residual feeling of doubt about your partner arises. I do not need to get into details with some of the other issues that would be created from these scenarios, but you can probably imagine what they are.

Let's take a closer look at what the Bible says about intimacy and what effects it has. God first created everything we know in the material and immaterial universe (Genesis 1:1). That intimate relationship was broken because of sin. God created a covenant that established a relationship with a people group that He created, the Hebrews, who would later make up the nation of Israel and would be called Jews. They were not able to live up to their end of the covenant relationship. A covenant was an agreement in the ancient world that created a relationship with stipulations for both parties involved. The Jews consistently did not live up to their end of the agreement and had to be corrected and brought back. They were eventually conquered and enslaved by the Babylonians because of their disobedience. God promised a new covenant though, that was not written on a scroll or on stone tablets but on people's hearts (Jeremiah 31:33). This was fulfilled through Christ and was initiated through His sacrifice, which gave forgiveness to all who would submit to Christ as their Lord, and believe that He was raised from the dead. This, in turn, cleared away all that was in the way of a truly intimate relationship with Him.

This removal of guilt allows the Holy Spirit to take up residence within us, giving us a new heart (Ezekiel 36:26). We are called to live in absolute union with Him (John 15:5), which creates the joy and freedom, in ever-increasing measure, that is associated with knowing a perfectly loving, joyful, peaceful, and perfect God. Man started out in an intimate relationship with God and broke that, but then God initiated a relationship with man through temporary covenants. He could have just broken up with us and forgot all about us. He didn't, though; He created a way for us to have an even closer relationship with Him through His Son Jesus. It is so close that we take on the very nature of God Himself. Did you ever notice that you begin to pick up the habits of those that you spend the most time with? This is what is happening here, except it is not picking up just the habits of God, but His very character.

Gospel Realities

The best is yet to come. As intimate as we can be with God now, these are all but illustrations of the real thing to come. God will continue to initiate a closer relationship with us. He will bring a city down from heaven where we cannot only live with God (Revelation 21:2), but we can see His face and know Him fully in ever-increasing measure (1 Corinthians 13:12, Revelation 22:4). We will do many of the same things we do now, but they will be uncorrupted by the destructive nature of sin and will come with the vibrancy and exuberance of walking with God in a depth of intimacy not yet fathomed by man. Do you see the pattern? God is always drawing closer to us. He is drawing near in this grand narrative, and is waiting for us to draw near to Him, and for us to know Him on a personal level (James 4:8).

This is what the entire pattern of Scripture is trying to illustrate to us. The whole of the Bible can be summed up in the word "relationship." A relationship comes with intimacy, struggles, difficulties, and joy. This is the relationship between God and man. All the positives of this list come from God, and all the negatives from man. It sounds cynical, but this is the power of sin and we must be aware of the reality where sin has placed us. God desires to replace all the baggage that sin carries with the nature of God Himself, with His "…love, joy, peace, patience, kindness, goodness, faithfulness, gentleness and self-control…." (Galatians 5:22-23). Do any of those characteristics bring burdens? No, they bring freedom.

How can there be so much evil in the world when there is a God like this? This evil is not from God but from sin. The very reason we die is because of sin (Romans 5:12). The reason death bothers us so much is because we were not designed for it. It brings problems. It brings sadness. It brings heartache and hardship. In the same way that sex outside of a covenant relationship brings problems, so does death. We were designed for neither of these. We did not have these problems before man sinned. You might say, "that was Adam so why do I suffer for that guy's disobedience?" Try to go one hour without sinning. Try to go five minutes without a sinful action, word or thought. We need a Savior. We need our character to be fundamentally transformed. That is what Christ has done. He made a way for us when all we ever tried to do was create barriers between Him and us. He died so that we could have life.

He made a way for us to live outside of those barriers that death and sin bring (John 3:16). When two people come together in intimacy, children are created. When God and man come together in intimacy, there is also new birth. A new person is created because a new nature is given. The old one is completely gone (2 Corinthians 5:17). The old person does not vanish, but he no longer holds power over you. You can be a new person because a new nature is given to you.

Gospel Realities

Chapter 16

A Living Story

God was drawing me closer to Himself throughout the course of my life. He said He would (John 12:32). We had a relationship in the beginning of my life that was separated because of sin, which created distance between us. God then revealed who He was to me before I stepped into this covenant. (Exodus 33). He had to release me from my life in captivity through miracles that broke the enemy's hold on me, just like He did with the Hebrews in Egypt. He led me out and revealed Himself to me. He set me on a journey that would consist of many battles just like the Hebrews fought, and will eventually bring me to a country that is not my own (Hebrews 11:14). Now I am a person called by this same God to "proclaim the excellencies of him who called you out of darkness and into his marvelous light" (1 Peter 2:9).

Many people have problems with believing one person's experience, and for good reason. People have the habit of embellishing, romanticizing, forgetting, or just outright deceiving people. They may have a story, but it can be polluted. I tell you my story and share my experience because it is not my own. It is part of a much larger story. I am a paragraph in a much larger book that I am not writing. My experiences are part of the story that the Bible has already written. What I have shared has been illustrated in that book long before I ever came about.

Many people love to look up into the starry sky at night. The universe is a beautiful, vast, dangerous, and wondrous place. It is filled with sights and sounds so great and beautiful that I can hardly fathom them. Many of them, I will never see in this temporal body. Those that live apart from God look up to the sky and see the same things. They see a vast sky with the same beautiful sights that I can see. They look up at the universe and feel very small. They feel that this universe is very impersonal. It can cause us to feel overwhelmed, alone, and insignificant.

When I look up, I see the beauty of God that is far beyond my comprehension. He is a God so beautiful that no earthly language can describe Him, and only metaphors can depict Him (Revelation 4). The universe draws me closer to this God because by seeing its beauty, I can see His beauty. If we were aliens, transported to Earth, and saw the inside of a computer, or a painting, or a busy highway full of automobiles, we could see more of what humanity is and what man is capable of. The same is true when we look at the vastness of space and realize the incredible nature of God.

The universe does not feel cold and impersonal to me anymore, because I know the God who created it is warm and very personal. I know that one day, in the new heavens, I may explore this universe without the limitations that this body now has. I will see what God has created and worship him more fully because of it. Now I look up and thank God for what He has made because I now know Him and everything He has created is interpreted through that lens.

The "weird" feeling that my friend Peter felt was the Holy Spirit. He felt the personal touch of God in Him. He felt the love of God being poured into his heart (Romans 5:5). He had an experience that was not a whimsical, emotionally induced experience, but the very thing that God said in His word that we would experience. Jesus said this about His resurrection: "And now I have told you before it takes place, so that when it does take place you may believe" (John 14:29). That is what He does with us. He reveals these things in His Bible so that, when they really happen to us, they give us perspective about what they really are. My story does not have to be the only thing to convince you, but it can help shape your story. Your story may consist of a different beginning and even a middle, but if you are reading this, then your end is not here yet.

It is not insignificant to be a paragraph in a much larger book. Your story can become one of the many paragraphs in a book much greater than any book you could ever write on your own. I may never write like C.S. Lewis, but his stories can help shape mine. Jesus is called "the author and perfecter of faith" (Hebrews 12:2 NASB). Jesus writes, not just a book filled with words, but with living illustrations and experiences. He is not limited in the way I am with

Gospel Realities

words and illustrations, but He is writing a story that is shaping your faith. Many people reading this already have this faith. Many do not. You are presently being drawn to Jesus. It is not by chance that you are reading this book. Each one of these chapters have experiences from my life that I have shared with you, and you are assimilating them into yours somehow and on varying levels. What would someone read about your life if you were to write your own story? Would it help someone else? How would it affect their life? You can write a new chapter in your own life today by giving your heart to Jesus.

Your choice will no doubt create heartache and hardship. It will be brutal. You will sacrifice, you will be persecuted, and you will be hated by many, but you will be loved by the Author. Stepping into the light means you become an enemy of those in darkness, demons, and any man that hates God. If you repent and accept Jesus as your Lord and Savior, a new paragraph in Jesus's book of faith will be revealed to you. Your paragraph will fit into His story. You will be created a new person, as the heavens and earth will be made new as well (Isaiah 65:17). All you have to do is change your mind about your sin, admit that it is sinful and separating you from God, and believe that He came and died for your sins. If you are reading this, "…now is the day of salvation…." (2 Corinthians 6:2). It is really that simple. If you genuinely gave your life to Jesus just now, your story has just taken a dramatic turn.

A Living Story

Why does God do it this way? Why does God lead us on a journey instead of just zapping us with all the truth and knowledge we need to be saved? Better yet, why doesn't He just come down and show Himself to us? You recall the story of the three wise men in the Bible (Matthew 2:1-12). They were also called Magi and the Bible makes a point to call them "wise." They were most likely from the area of Mesopotamia, so they had to make a journey that would have been of some length. We do not know much about these particular Magi, but we do know they were led supernaturally, by a star, to the location of Jesus's birth.

They had come from a place of darkness to a place where the True Light was shining. They were led by a star to the location of Jesus. They had to physically travel from one location to another being led by this star with supernatural direction. They immediately recognized the divinity of Jesus and came to pay the proper respect to the King. What is unique about these journeys that God takes us on is not always the blatantly supernatural beginnings and endings, but all the stuff that happens in between. It's kind of like a sandwich. You know what type of sandwich you are eating by what is in the middle of it. That's where the good stuff is.

These men were traveling a great distance, just enough distance to allow room for discouragement, doubt, or uncertainty to set in. We do not know what particular emotions these Magi faced, but we do know they were continually led to the exact location of the manger where Jesus lay. These men were gentiles; they were foreigners to the nation of Israel. Still, at the very onset of Jesus's life here on earth, they were drawn to Him. Isaiah 60:3 says, "And nations shall come to your light, and kings to the brightness of your rising." Isaiah here is referencing Jesus. There are countless times in Scripture where God is depicted as light. Revelation 22:16 says, "I, Jesus, have sent my angel to testify to you about these things for the churches. I am the root and the descendant of David, the bright morning star." In John 1:4-5, we read, "In him was life, and the life was the light of men. The light shines in the darkness, and the darkness has not overcome it." 1 John 1:5 proclaims, "This is the message we have heard from him and proclaim to you, that God is light, and in him is no darkness at all." These are just a few verses of many. The Bible makes it very clear that God is light.

I am not referring to God being light in a physical sense, but in the spiritual sense. The spiritual is not some spooky or whimsical otherworld dimension, but the very source of all things that have been created. God Himself is spirit: "God is spirit, and those who worship him must worship in spirit and truth" (John 4:24).

This has been one of the central themes I have tried to illustrate in this book, and that is that everything good that is created in the physical world, is merely a reflection of a much greater reality in the spiritual world. The origin of all things is not in the physical world, but in the spiritual: "All things were made through him, and without him was not anything made that was made" (John 1:3).

This seems strange or foreign to us because all we can see with our physical eyes is the physical universe. Of course, there would be limitations to that. That does not mean that is all there is. God has left us clues about Himself and the reality of His Kingdom all over the place. For instance, in the absence of light, man is naturally blind. It is not the physical eye alone that allows us to see. It takes light entering through the pupil to illuminate an object and allow a man to see what is in front of him. That is why, when you are in a room where no outside light can get in and you turn the lights off, you can see nothing. The absence of light creates blindness, as we might perceive it, but, in reality, it is merely the natural condition we are all in without light.

The same is true in the spiritual kingdom as well. We have been living in a "kingdom of darkness" (Colossians 1:13). We all would be blind to the truth of God without Him giving us light. Just as we cannot physically see without light, we also cannot spiritually see without light. People search hard for God in various religions. Some look for some sort of experience as proof. Experience is important in one's relationship with God, but this light is not directing us to some whimsical God or to an experience by itself. We are being directed to Jesus Christ.

Many look for God in some big experience, refusing to look for Him in everyday details. If we only look for God in the big things, then we are missing so much of who God really is. He is not just the God of the big; He is also the God of the small. He created

Gospel Realities

both. Your life is not an accident, coincidence, or mistake. No matter how many times you or someone else has told you that. You were placed here on earth for a reason. Psalm 139:16 says, "Your eyes saw my unformed substance; in your book were written, every one of them, the days that were formed for me, when as yet there was none of them." This verse reminds you, that before you began to develop in your mother's womb, God knew exactly what you would look like. Before you ever woke up and lived any of your days, God had already written your life story.

Chapter 17
New You = New Goal

Some reading this have led a life of great pain, and that has not escaped God's books, nor has it been useless. Some have led a life of great comfort. Neither does that lack a purpose. The person that makes all that "stuff" fall into its proper perspective is Christ. Many people strive for some goal in their life without Christ. They may strive for comfort. They may strive for money or sex. They may strive to be as learned as possible. They may make that their goal, only to find it is not fulfilling. Or they may not attain it and always be disappointed.

    Whether they achieve it or not, they are left unfulfilled. I have met people who seek money constantly, but, when they get all they want, they are still bankrupt. There are people that strive for relationships with people. They already have many relationships, but always need more, or maybe the ones they have are never quite right. Where is the end to this never-ending cycle? No one living outside of Christ has ever answered that question. If it had, the world would be a radically different place. If it had, religion, and not just Christianity would have disappeared long ago. Consumerism would diminish and not increase like it has been because people would be fulfilled. Poverty would no longer hold its power.

Yet as it is, no one outside of Christ has discovered it yet. We are looking to fulfill this thirst in ourselves. John 4:14 says, "but whoever drinks of the water that I will give him will never be thirsty again…" We look for things in the physical world to satisfy us, but it is only what is found in the spiritual that can satisfy our thirst. The apostle Paul made a statement about his life's goal that put for him, and anyone else that shares it, man's thirst into its proper place. This verse takes our thirst, and re-orients it to a place that is no longer destructive, but healing. It no longer deceives us by promising fulfillment and coming up short, but actually fulfills. Christ fuels the fire of man's hunger, directs it, fulfills it, and burns up anything that stands in the way of it. Paul said this: "That I may know Him and the power of His resurrection and the fellowship of His sufferings, being conformed to His death" (Philippians 3:10 NASB).

In the passage preceding this verse, Paul listed many things that would have been counted as supreme worth in the culture of his time. He said they had no value compared to knowing Christ. In this verse, Paul listed the priorities in his life: 1) knowing Christ, 2) knowing the power of His resurrection, 3) sharing His sufferings. God was not only specific about what words went into His Word, but also where they were placed. This list tells us that Paul's first priority was knowing Christ. It was to walk in intimacy with Him, and to discover who He was in all things.

This priority comes first because this is what the other two are about as well. Knowing Christ allows us to discover the power of His resurrection, which is the power of the Holy Spirit that was at work within Paul. This power is also released in us so that we might know Him. Then there comes the "kicker"—sharing in His sufferings. Paul so wished to know Christ that he wanted to suffer like Christ. He knew this would open the door for more intimacy with Him, and that intimacy would transform Paul himself into like nature with Christ. Paul's first priority was knowing Christ, and the other two are ways for that to happen. They are included in the package deal of knowing Christ.

All these things placed the events of Paul's life into proper perspective. Paul was someone who carried the Gospel to many areas in the ancient world. He suffered persecution, abandonment, treachery, and experienced miracles, all of which created an incredible intimacy between Him and God. He knew what it meant to know Christ, His power, and His sufferings. He had walked through many trials in his life, and knew Christ was in them all.

All our life events need to fit into this proper paradigm in order for them to fulfill their purpose. We were created to know Christ for eternity, not just here and now. We will spend an eternity discovering Him, even after sin, death, and the opportunity to repent are gone. God is self-sufficient, self-sustaining, and can never be exhausted, so we will always be on a journey to discover and grow in this intimacy with Him. We are not limited by sin's existence in

Gospel Realities

knowing God. Our intimacy will go on and on into eternity with Him. Paul's mission on earth was the same as it will be in Heaven. There is no suffering in the new heavens and the new Earth, but those sufferings were designed for us to have intimacy with God. This will never be an obsolete goal. Paul's goal is the goal of anyone currently in heaven and anyone in the new heavens and the new earth, and that is the pursuit of intimacy with God. Jesus prayed in Matthew 6:10, "your kingdom come, your will be done, on earth as it is in heaven." Just like everything that was created by God who is in heaven, our goal on earth will be the same goal in heaven.

In the Garden of Eden, there was no sin and death, yet there was intimacy with God. There was unhindered fellowship with Him. In pursuing God in intimacy, we are not creating a new goal, we are only going back to the original one. It was because of sin that we created new goals, agendas, and ways of conceptualizing life. We are only doing what we were created to do, and that will bring us fulfillment. What does that look like?

In the world of pastoral ministry, there is often a pollution of God's agenda in our own lives. Pastors want numbers, they want their members to give and to serve, and they want a healthy church. They want to preach great sermons and they want the lost to be saved. Those are all good things, but they become bad when we lose sight of their purpose. Instead of a growing church being about the overflow of your joy and fulfillment in God to others, it becomes about being the hottest church in the city. Instead of preaching a

New You = New Goal

great sermon to have intimacy with God, it becomes about a performance. The hermeneutical rules or the drama that accompanies preaching a sermon are good, but when those are not used to seek intimacy with God, and do not flow from intimacy with God, we become performing monkeys for the crowd instead of a vessel that honors God.

When we lose God's perspective for these things, which is always intimacy, we replace it, by default, with ours. We pray for a church and preach to win man's approval in hopes that that will give us fulfillment, but it never satisfies. This is pastoral ministry, a job that is supposed to be the most God-honoring in many people's eyes. People hold the bar incredibly high for pastors, and if it can happen in a pastorate, I am sure you can see how you, also, might be affected, no matter what your position.

We also cannot limit intimacy to just our professions. We cannot compartmentalize. Compartmentalization is what has polluted the allure of Christianity in general. So many people that are used to compartmentalizing their lives have taken Jesus and done the same thing with Him. Their lives are like filing cabinets, with a folder for each aspect of their lives. They have the wife folder. The children folder. The job folder. The hobbies folder. The list can go on and on and vary from person to person, but the principle still applies. When we put Jesus in a folder, it is usually a dusty old folder in the back of the filing cabinet, and that is not appealing at all. Our lives have enough tasks and we are busy enough in this country as it is. The

Gospel Realities

thought of one more folder makes many squirm. We will add that folder if it helps us to achieve the tasks in those other folders though. These are the people who only pray to God when they are in a bind and need help, or those that have bought in to the many claims of the prosperity Gospel. Jesus does not ask us to give him a folder, especially one that we only open on Christmas and Easter. That is not a real relationship anyway. He wants the entire "cabinet," our entire lives.

Jesus says in Luke 17:33, "Whoever seeks to preserve his life will lose it, but whoever loses his life will keep it." Jesus is using a traditional rabbinical technique of extremes to illustrate not survival, but surrender. Jesus says that whoever seeks to harness, protect, and keep locked behind closed doors, his own life, will wind up with nothing in it, but whoever surrenders his entire life to Jesus will get the very essence of life that will preserve him in eternity. God is always trying to expand our capacities to know Him, and that is what I am hoping to do in this book as well. The more we surrender our own perceptions to Christ, the more we will be enlightened. We were meant to find God in every aspect of our lives, not just at church, or in books, or Christian music. We can, of course, find Him in these things, but He wants us to find Him in everything.

He wants us to find Him in a beautiful day, a cool breeze, and a starry night sky. He wants us to find Him behind our desk at work or in a manufacturing plant working on a machine. He wants us to find Him in our relationships. That includes our friendships, our marriage, our girlfriends or boyfriends, and even our singleness. He wants us to find Him in our beautiful children, our obnoxious co-worker, and our aunt Sally. He wants us to find Him in our tears, our laughter, our dreams, and our goals for the future. He wants us to find Him in our joy, and our pain. He wants us to find Him in our hopelessness and our hope.

Some of these things are not good, but they are meant to point us to the One that is. If you do not believe me, take in the beauty of this verse. "For by him all things were created, in heaven and on earth, visible and invisible, whether thrones or dominions or rulers or authorities-all things were created through him and for him" (Colossians 1:16). Did you catch that last part? Everything was created by Him and for Him. That means that we can see Christ in everything because He either created it or allowed it to happen. There is evidence all around us.

We get caught up in God's creative work by being given opportunity to see Him in what He has created, which fulfills its purpose, which was for us to know Him, thus glorifying Him. How much evidence does it take to convince a jury and make a case? A few eyewitnesses? Jesus has left millions of eyewitnesses throughout history and the sky we look up to at night at as well: "The heavens declare the glory of God, and the sky proclaims his handiwork" (Psalm 19:1).

Every day and night, we are faced with evidence. We are facing a reality that the Bible tells us we are in. When those two come

Gospel Realities

together, faith is created. When those two are separated in us is where unbelief defines us. Faith has been called many things. It has been called wishful thinking, a crutch, stupidity, an overcomer, and the "assurance of things hoped for" (Hebrews 11:1). Faith really acts best as a bridge that connects us to God. It is what connects the hope that He gives us. It gives us the power to press on in difficulties and storms. It gives us joy in any circumstance and it changes our perspective. Faith creates a bridge between our reality and God's. When those two collide, we realize the magnitude of God's reality, and His reality becomes ours. Faith is what enables us to step out of our reality and step into God's. The truth is that His reality has always been the real one, and faith is what gives us the eyes to see it.

If you and I had no faith in Christ, your reality would not be mine. The sense that truth is relative is slightly true, except that it is not really our truth that is relative, just our perception. Our days would look different. I would get up and go to work at a certain time, come home at a certain time, spend time with certain people and you would do something like this with different variables. You would see the world differently than me because of your perception. Outside of faith, we would both belong to God's reality. We would both relate to God in a similar fashion, which is not at all. The activities of our day would look different, but we would still fall under the umbrella of God's reality. When God's kingdom comes down on us, we see it for what it is. We see what is behind the scenes in our lives. We discover the source of our hurts, our hopelessness, and our own selfishness.

New You = New Goal

We wake up and see what has been created around us as being created for us, not just to see but to see through.

If someone is lying to us and we instinctively know it, we will say we can see right through the lie. Maybe the lie in this case is not believing that what has been created around you is designed for us to see through so we can see the truth. Jesus said of Himself, "...I am the way and truth and the life. No one comes to the Father except through me" (John 14:6). 2 Corinthians 4:18 says, "as we look not to the things that are seen but to the things that are unseen. For the things that are seen are transient, but the things that are unseen are eternal." How are we to see something that is unseen? The Bible is not telling us to look with our physical eyes, but with our spiritual ones. With faith, we are able to see the unseen. We are able to look beyond what we see to see why we see it. So, nature and our relationships are not an end to themselves like so many of us make them, but they are meant for us to see beyond them to the source of Who created the stars and Who created relationships.

When we examine them properly and see the unseen beyond the seen, then we engage in what is seen differently. Let's look at the most sought-after thing in all the world. Some find it and some never do, but all of us crave it, and that is love. Love is something that is possible, but can be polluted. We search for love in things instead of people, and we get hurt. We can give our spouse a selfish love that brings only benefits for ourselves. For those who see Christ, we begin to see love for what it really is. 1 John 4:8 says that "...God is love." God is the very essence of love itself. It is found in Him. Anytime we express it, it is because it is from Him. When we see love in God, we engage others with the same love. We understand that "We love because He first loved us." (1 John 4:19) When we believe in Him, we begin to love others in the same way. It becomes our motivation, and it moves us forward. God's love is not dependent on circumstance, it does not fluctuate, and it is not whimsical. It is rock solid, steady, and not earned. It is merely revealed through Christ. It has always been demonstrated through Christ.

We love others depending on situations. It depends on time, our mood, and whether we feel like it. God's love in us is a river that never stops. If we do not dam it with sin, then it flows through us and into others. We can engage others with unconditional love because we have not fixed our eyes on the temporary conditions of a finite love, but on the unseen and unconditional source of love. We always give it because we always have it. It never leaves us because it has been "poured into our hearts" (Romans 5:5). Since it has been poured into us, we carry it around with us. We are vessels that take it into any situation. It is there when we talk to any person. It is there when others demonstrate their hate for us. It is there when the wounds of the past cry out for us to indulge them. It is there in the morning. It is there in the evening. It is there when we stare into the sky and it is there when we sleep. It is there because God is always there.

New You = New Goal

How radical is that? Our world is crying out for love now. Turn on your news for a while. Watch the protests, the hate, the terrorism, the brutality of those in just our country, let alone elsewhere. We need it now and we have always needed it. If the world knew the love of Christ, it would be radically different. It would not feel so cold, estranged, distant, or gray, but it would be alive with a radical vibrancy and life.

That gray perspective is now gone in me. When I discovered Christ, that vibrancy and light came into me. Now the world is brighter, full of colors I never knew existed. The light inside of me has illuminated the way I see the world. I have become a person who carries that light. I remember walking into a prayer meeting once and a man told me I was beaming with light and he could see it all over me. What I once recognized in others has become true of myself. Jesus says His followers are salt and light (Matthew 5:13-16). When I shine the light of God to others, I "season," or make more delicious, what would normally be a bland, empty existence. Some people hate it because they don't have it and do not want it; others come to it because of what it is. These are the people that we are called to be. We are called to be people transformed by the recognition of God's reality and, whatever place we enter, we are to transform as well.

This book will not give you all the illustrations we see in the natural of things that are the reality in the spirit. There is just not enough room in this book, nor could I ever hope to harness all the manifold wisdom of God. I am still constantly surprised by the

Gospel Realities

depths of His wisdom. Even this very day, I am discovering just how deep His wisdom is in the everyday scruples of life and how widely it is revealed in every facet of creation. What I do want to look at some more are two clearly revealed acts in the Bible that demonstrate this principle. The first is baptism.

The act of baptism is an invitation to participate in one of God's great illustrations. When we confess Christ as our Lord and Savior and trust in Him to forgive us of our sins, there is both death and life at work in you at the same time. The death that occurs is the death of your old sinful nature. This death does not mean it goes away, but the old you does. The old you was the person you were before Christ, totally captivated and swayed by your sin while being blind to your very pitiful condition. That part of you no longer remains the standard default by which you operate. You are given a new nature. You are given the very nature of God himself and that happens after you are born again. Paul says in 2 Corinthians 5:17, "Therefore, if anyone is in Christ, he is a new creation. The old has passed away; behold, the new has come." The old you dies and the new you is born, the part of you that has the very essence of eternal life in it. The part that is born is the nature in you that can live by the Spirit of God, instead of being dominated by your sinful passions.

When you are baptized, you are symbolically showing in the physical what has happened in the spiritual. We cannot witness the greatness of that instantaneous death and life in you, but, through baptism, we are invited to see the metaphorical death as you are

New You = New Goal

immersed underwater and raised up again to symbolize how you have been raised up with Christ. The spiritual activity does not happen in that moment. In fact, it already happened when you submitted to Christ, but you are demonstrating to others after the fact what He has already done. The wedding ring is a common illustration. You are not married because you have a ring, but you wear the ring because you are married. The ring becomes a symbol of the marriage, just as baptism becomes a symbol of your "resurrection."

Another activity we participate in is the Lord's Supper. This is a little different in a sense, but the principle of illustration still applies. As followers of Christ, we designate a time during our worship services to eat some form of bread and drink a cup of either wine or grape juice. Jesus, at the Last Supper, did this with His disciples shortly before He was to be crucified. Jesus commanded them to "…do this in remembrance of me." (1 Corinthians 11:24) and so we continue to do so.

We eat the bread and drink the cup as illustrations of the reality that Christ really did give up His body and pour out His blood for the forgiveness of our sins. We do this to illustrate how we share in the giving of His body and pouring out of His blood by the reaping of those benefits in our lives. We live in eternal forgiveness because of the one-time act of ultimate sacrifice that Jesus performed for us. We are called to participate in the demonstration of that reality.

So we are called not only to recognize the reality of God's kingdom in our lives, we are called to participate. Maybe called is not a strong enough word; we are commanded. That word brings a harsh connotation for it with those who haven't learned completely the nature of God's commands. Commands are given for us to participate in the illustrations God gives of Himself to others and ourselves. For instance, we are commanded to love God completely and others like ourselves (Matthew 22:36-40). Why do we do that? We do that because "God is love." (1 John 4:8) and "We love because he first loved us" (1 John 4:19). We are called to participate in the nature of God Himself out of the overflow of how He is transforming us into people with the same nature as Christ (2 Corinthians 3:18). The ultimate command of Christ was that He was to be crucified for us. He did it "for the joy that was set before him" (Hebrews 12:2). His command from the Father was for His joy, and so is ours. We are commanded to partake in God's joy. If you don't love joy, His commands will always prove to be burdensome, but for those that do, His joy for you is not even an option. It is something you will and must have as His follower. The fruit of the Spirit is "love, joy…" (Galatians 5:22). The parable of the faithful servant tells us to be faithful in what God has given us. Our faithfulness is not an option; it is a command from God:

> For it will be like a man going on a journey, who called his servants and entrusted to them his property. To one he gave five talents, to another two, to another one, to each according

New You = New Goal

to his ability. Then he went away. He who had received the five talents went at once and traded with them, and he made five talents more. So also he who had the two talents made two talents more. But he who had received the one talent went and dug in the ground and hid his master's money. Now after a long time the master of those servants came and settled accounts with them. And he who had received the five talents came forward, bringing five talents more, saying, 'Master, you delivered to me five talents; here, I have made five talents more.' His master said to him, 'Well done, good and faithful servant. You have been faithful over a little; I will set you over much. Enter into the joy of your master.' And he also who had the two talents came forward, saying, 'Master, you delivered to me two talents; here, I have made two talents more.' His master said to him, 'Well done, good and faithful servant. You have been faithful over a little; I will set you over much. Enter into the joy of your master.' He also who had received the one talent came forward, saying, 'Master, I knew you to be a hard man, reaping where you did not sow, and gathering where you scattered no seed, so I was afraid, and I went and hid your talent in the ground. Here, you have what is yours.' But his master answered him, 'You wicked and slothful servant! You knew that I reap where I have not sown and gather where I scattered no seed? Then you ought to have invested my money with the bankers, and at my coming I should have received what was my own with interest. So take the talent from him and give it to him who has the ten talents. For to everyone who has will more be given, and he will have an abundance. But from the one who has not, even what he has will be taken away. And cast the worthless servant into the outer darkness. In that place there will be weeping and gnashing of teeth (Matthew 25:14-30)

We tend to think of being faithful in this passage in terms of teaching Sunday school, or showing up to work on time every day. If we view it like that, we limit our view of God's kingdom in our lives and we limit our joy. The "talents" that these servants are given in the Greek is money, and is the english word for our God-given abilities. That is some ironic wording if you ask me! This passage not only applies to our money, but our gifts and talents.

If God has given you a gift to paint, you are commanded to do so! If you are given a gift in public speaking, you are commanded to speak! If you sing, you are to sing, if you write you are to write, if math you are to use it, if serving, then serve! God is telling us to work out what He has worked in! The gifts and talents God gives are ones that we enjoy if used for God's kingdom. We might not always like the act itself, but we will enjoy finding God in those things! Remember, all of what we were created for, along with our gifts and talents, are for living in intimacy with God. You might not like your job, even if you are gifted in it, but discovering God through your gift is what makes it enjoyable. I have worked jobs I have hated, and I have worked jobs I love, which includes my current one! I have discovered God in both.

What we tend to lose sight of in our gifts are their very purpose. We fail to lose sight that each one of those gifts are merely the manifestation of God Himself in that area of gifting. If you serve, it is because, "even as the son of Man came not to be served but to serve..." (Matthew 20:28). If you paint, it is because God is the greatest artist of all time. He not only manipulates what He created for beauty, he creates ex-nihilo, which means "out of nothing" (Genesis 1:1). If you preach, it is because God is the greatest communicator of Himself there ever was. That is revealed to us in all sixty-six books of the Bible.

We live not by coincidence, but as Jesus said in John 14:19, "Because I live, you also will live." We breathe because God breathed the very breath of life into us (Genesis 2:7, Acts 17:25). Everything we are is because He was first, from the top down, from the gifts we have to our very existence. Everything is an illustration. Even if you fall asleep sometimes when your pastor is preaching, you still can't miss the sermon, God Himself is preaching to you before and after it. There is nowhere you can run to hide from God's revelation about Himself. The very ground you stand on was created by Him (Genesis 1:1).

We are held accountable for what we do with what we have been given. We answer to God for our talents. Those servants whose

Gospel Realities

identity was good and faithful lived it out and were rewarded with joy. The wicked one who despised his Master and His gift was tossed into a place where everything was full of darkness and pain and where God was absent. God is light and healing, and if we spurn Him, we wind up without His goodness for eternity. Do not fall asleep during God's sermon. Whether you sleep through it or listen and are engaged, you are still held accountable for it.

I like to tell a story that makes me laugh, but also reminds me of God's sovereignty. When I was in high school, I used to say I would never get married and have kids. God was also the furthest thing from my mind. Here I am now, twenty-seven and married with three kids. I drive a minivan and I am a pastor. God never does things the way I foresee them, and I am glad. His plan was much better than mine. I have found joy unlike anything I have ever known. I have peace like I have never known. I have trial like I have never known either, but now I know the One from Whom this incredible joy, peace, and endurance in difficulty comes. I know God the Father, through Jesus Christ, and I am filled with the Holy Spirit.

Conclusion

I would have never believed this would have been my future. Who can even guess such a thing? I know where I have been, I know where I am now, but I do not know my near future. I do not know what tomorrow holds, but I know Who holds it. The same God who was in charge of my past is in charge of my future. I have seen what He can do throughout the years. He let me go through incredible pain in order to find Him. Now that I know Him, I would not have chosen any other way. The Bible says, "For I consider that the sufferings of this present time are not worth comparing with the glory that is to be revealed to us" (Romans 8:18). This verse talks about the glory awaiting us when we are in Heaven, but also applies to us now. Knowing Christ is worth all the suffering that is to come, even the suffering that comes as a consequence of knowing Him.

Those cries that I spoke about in the beginning of the book are not cries of pain. They were, but not anymore. They are cries of hope. Romans 8:23 says, "And not only the creation, but we ourselves, who have the first fruits of the Spirit, groan inwardly as we wait eagerly for the adoption as sons, the redemption of our bodies." Those cries are inward groans. They are signs that I have not been created for a sinful world and my very being is crying out for the glory that is awaiting me. I do not belong here. That is good and not bad. I belong in the New Earth and not the old. This is good because now I can live like I am created for a better earth. I take the reality of that and live it out here on an Earth that is still full of pain, agony, suffering, and God's beauty. I bring light into the darkness and hope to those without hope. I cry not from pain, but from joy. My creation has joy now but longs for the greater joy found in the glory that is to come. I have my feet on the ground and my head is in heaven, and because of that, I am stretched. All that is stretched is filled in with God. I do not even know what this evening will hold, but I know God is there, and that is enough for me.

Notes

Introduction:

[1] Brian Davies, *The Thought of Thomas Aquinas* (Oxford: Oxford University Press, 1992) 9.

Chapter 2: Some Things You Can't Control

[2] C.S. Lewis, *Mere Christianity*, (New York: Broadman and Holman Publishers, 1996) 121.

Chapter 10: The Only Way Out

[3] *The Matrix*. Dir. Lana Wachowski and Lilly Wachowski. Warner Bros, 1999.

Made in the USA
Middletown, DE
05 April 2018